# Natural Justice

# -

# Economic Satyagraha

Rob Grosche

# DEDICATION

*To V. Kalynam and Anna Hazare*

*who still brightly carry the Satyagraha torch in 2012.*

*...and to Ela Gandhi and many other contributors whose encouragement and knowledge enriched this book.*

*Foremost also hugs to my family for putting up with me during my epic struggle and long absences to complete these books.*

*"We cannot and must not let our humanity be traded for profit. Socrates lived in a barrel and walked at night the streets shining a lantern into stranger's eyes looking for an honest man.*

*We too must look into ourselves and find that lost dignity and honor.*

*Being honorable and noble has nothing to do with being royal but with the other meaning of noble, which is based on how charitably and upright you interact with others. Being noble, doing what is right irrespective of how hard it is, is being truly noble. Today however being noble has been replaced with being rich, and rich people are being revered as gods, while good people are looked at as quirky... like mother Theresa, Bono and Geldorf."*

Veit Grosche 2006, Humanist.

*"Where justice is denied, where poverty is enforced, where ignorance prevails, and where any one class is made to feel that society is in an organised conspiracy to oppress, rob, and degrade them, neither persons nor property will be safe."*

Frederick Douglass, abolitionist and statesman, Speech, April 1886

# Table of Contents

# *Acknowledgments*

————————

*Ideas are sparked by interacting with people and fine-tuned by experience and criticism.*

*I would like to thank everyone who has contributed to this book.*

*Especially, I would like to single out my brother Veit, who has been a ruthless critic and has stuck with this project from its beginnings.*

*Deserving of an endurance medal is my wife Michele who not only helped me to focus intellectually, but also carried me and my selfish ambitions though thick and thin.*
*My immediate family and friends, past and present, who are keen intellects and moral fortresses, have also been formidable critics and frequently unwitting contributors and co-writers.*

# ABOUT THE AUTHOR

Rob is a child of post war Germany. Educated and raised in Frankfurt am Main.

He was too young to remember the hip sixties and too innocent and too busy struggling to become an optician to fully grasp why his university educated Zeitgenossen ripped up cobblestones as missiles and hurled them in pitch battles at the police.

All-the while Bader Meinhof tried to bomb the establishment and impoverished GI's rioted in US barracks fearing their deployment in Vietnam. Ho Ho Ho Chi Minh was the battle cry of the discontented and red stars and red revolutionaries were the favorite T-shirt logos worn with bell bottom trousers, revolutionary loud music and girlish long or Afro bouffed hair.

Bewildered not only by Hitlers legacy, the Vietnam war and the delights and terrors of girls he ended up working as a union steel man in Port Kembla Australia. There he misspent the remainder of his youth learning English, loving, body surfing, tanning and bush walking.

Today he is married, still working in optics, still loves his adopted Australia and runs a number of very small companies and research/incubator companies which have a social slant.

Protest is good!

# *Preamble*

Action – not words – conquers all!

There has never been a statue erected to a person who lived a quiet peaceful life.

The earth that the meek will inherit is a world of wars, poverty, hunger, and a meaningless life of drudgery. Whether they live on the streets, in a tin shed in the slums or in an over-mortgaged, over-valued brick veneer bungalow in the outer suburbs, they will always live far away from the seats of power, fun and frivolity. That is the way it has always been and the way it will be for all time to come …until we change meekness into action and fearful acceptance of our situation into active rage!

We ourselves, our writers, journalists, politicians and artists have observed, commented and lamented the poor state of our planet and the diabolical inhumanity that drives our affairs. Yes, we observe, but in truth, our outrage is mostly just hot air and cheap talk!

So why does anyone still bother to be outraged at injustice? Why is the common spark that burns at the heart of our humanity wounded when we witness suffering? Why don't we just give up and let all this evil, filth and injustice wash over us in a tidal wave of indifference?

*Economic Satyagraha* explores profound moral questions, but, unlike most books that bemoan events, this series explores the causes of our moral discontent and, above all, offers realistic moral alternatives, which conjure up a *Zeitgeist* from a distinctly personal perspective that you can own.

Humanity's epic journey from slime to paradise looks increasingly like ending in *Terminus* oblivion rather than heaven on earth. This is why the Economic Satyagraha series tries to prick our smug conscience by suggesting realistic alternatives to our schizoid mass media-taught morals.

The books are serious in nature, but also try to entertain a little – a dangerous mix as they walk a fine line between entertainment, an exploration of historic precedents, righteous anger, outrage and ridicule.

Hopefully, these books can make us think about altering our society's destructive course by exploring a realistic alternative reality – one that we can personally embrace both with our head and with our heart. More importantly they are written because we know deep inside that we *can* create a new world without hunger, poverty and war. But we also know instinctively, that we hate change and most of us are ok with the world, just the way it is, because we don't feel deprived personally.

But, unless meek couch potatoes like you and me, pub politicians, aloof university boffins, slum princes and princesses and ideological malcontents begin to act on their righteous indignation and actually begin to do something other than talk and write, nothing will ever change!

Reality and news media fiction are daily mixing us a heady cocktail of fear, anger and blind hate. Humanity appears locked into ever more angry confrontations that appear to be out of control.

Peace is not the absence of war, but a constant struggle for good. War, on the other hand, is the absence of love, reason and compassion. Unless good people act, it will be the dying of the light. We know it.

Dylan Thomas when he penned: *"Rage, rage against the dying of the light."* knew it!

The world belongs to those who think and act.

NICE TRY... but I am not sure if anyone will remember the salient points of the message ... or if it will have the desired impact to rally anti-war supporters or if it will do anything to stop war.

# *Gravitas or grotesque?*

*"Peace should be understood in a human way − in a broad social, political and economic way. Peace is threatened by unjust economic, social and political order, absence of democracy, environmental degradation and absence of human rights.*

**Poverty is the absence of all human rights.**

*The frustrations, hostility and anger generated by abject poverty cannot sustain peace in any society. For building stable peace we must find ways to provide opportunities for people to live decent lives. "*

Muhammad Yunus Nobel Peace Prize 2006

_____

Like me, you might once have expressed outrage over an injustice, only to be put in your place with a comment such as "And what gives you the right to complain?"

Whoever made that comeback had a really good point. Just because we feel strongly about something, does not mean that this emotion is grounded in logic or facts sufficiently strongly to excuse or justify a raucous, indignant outburst. Therefore it follows that when we take a stand against something, we should be able to intellectually defend it and be very sure that our indignation has a solid and justifiable foundation in logic and fact, rather than emotionally charged, blind indignation.. Still most of us just have a gut instinct that something is wrong, but we still claim what Gandhi calls *"...the right to conscience without going through any discipline whatsoever..."*

A gut instinct just won't do when we argue matters of justice, war, life and death. If we want to succeed and be taken seriously, we need to underpin our indignation with something that resembles gravitas instead of happy-hippy fluff.

Today, some of us can give our arguments and indignation weight merely by displaying conspicuous wealth, by exercising raw powers, by holding celebrity status or by enjoying notoriety. But in the absence of those advantages, our arguments have to be underpinned by irrefutable facts and sound reason, as we ordinary people have no credibility privileges!

In the absence of one or more of these criteria, our outrage rings hollow because we, the readers of this book, live in a good-time culture that underpins its wealthy lifestyle by keeping four billion people in poverty and slave-like servitude whilst one billion aspire to join the elite economies.

It is common knowledge that our planet can support a maximum of about 12 billion people, if we all lived the frugal lifestyle of a slum dweller, but only about 2 billion if we all lived the lifestyle of the British. Clearly - after doing the math - we have to keep 4 billion people in poverty. The next billion serves us as a protective defense and buffer zone from the poor. Like it or not, the facts show that unless we reduce our consumption and pay more for our goods which are produced by the poor, effectively re-distributing and sharing our good fortune and wealth with the poor, we have to keep exploiting them, to maintain our lifestyle!

This is a very grave point that can't be made strongly enough! We see daily, countless good people frustrated, wasting their efforts trying to change the world into a better place only to find ourselves cringing at their childish arguments. Or worse, we are ashamed because they fail to connect with a *Zeitgeist* that now finds it intolerable to see people starve to death a few flight hours out of London's Heathrow airport.

Ideas are powerful and words can cut through the media clutter, but only if they touch the core of our heart and wound our moral smugness and self-righteous beliefs.

Therefore, before we shout our beliefs from the rooftops, we should first prove, even if it is just to ourselves, that we are right and justified in our rage. This book explores how we can test our outrage and prove that we have taken an honest, defensible and effective position that unambiguously defines what is right and just and what is blatantly wrong and unjust. Before we cheapen a cause we believe in, by saying and doing stupid things, we owe it to the *Zeitgeist* that drives our desires and fuels our rage, to prepare ourselves.

We all know the feeling of rage that burns in our hearts when we witness an injustice, but what gives us this strong feeling and where does it come from? Sure, we were taught right from wrong as children and can form an opinion based on our experiences. But there appears to be a deeper force which drives our emotions. This force is hard to define; it is instinctive, genetic, primitive, and downright primeval. It is a flame that burns within and if we ignore it, it gnaws at our self-worth and opens a door to dark despair. It leaves us feeling helpless and our cause and struggle hopeless. Succeeding in a gigantic struggle for justice is a bit like eating a giant wedding cake. We can't eat it with a single bite, but rather one mouthful at a time, and we need a lot of hungry people to help us eat it before it goes off. In the absence of a hungry crowd, we need to take the long view and be prepared to work with determination, slowly, bite by bite, towards our objective.

# *What gives you the right to complain?*

---

*Could Winston Churchill ever foresee that a man he ridiculed for being non-violent and for wearing a cheesecloth nappy would one day defeat the military might of the world's largest, empire ever?*

There is a lot of noise being made about ending poverty and everyone seemingly has a quick-fix at the ready. But, in the end, after reality bites, we all feel a little powerless and overwhelmed by the scale of the problem and by the systemic methods which our society employs to sustain and profit from poverty.

Economic Satyagraha developed from the Gandhian ideology of Satyagraha. It has been adapted and reinterpreted so that it can be understood in our times. It connects seemingly unrelated issues to form a clear picture of how we got into this global mess and shows how we can get out of it. But most importantly a Satyagraha is a personal discovery of a deep truth that eventually allows us to act.  It is based on a righteous, logical foundation that strengthens our resolve to act, strong in the knowledge that our actions are just.

Economic Satyagraha's ideas are as old as time. In this book, I have simply fused Ghandi's Satyagraha ideologies and practical methods with various aspects of economics, history, religion and human rights, using a systems analyst's eye to develop workable solutions which could end poverty, hunger and wars forever. Having set the bar below Limbo's natural limits, let's see if the truth, just like the original Limbo dance, will set your conscience and curiosity free?

Economic Satyagraha is an old non-violent ideology adapted to our times and to our new understanding of world events. It empowers individuals to take charge of their own economic affairs in order to allow disadvantaged people to break away from poverty, gender inequality, environmental degradation, economically-based wars, wars in general, unjust monopolies, corporations, corrupt governments, power-hungry individuals and aggressive empires. These are big claims and it is understandable that we would want to test and verify their earnestness and validity before committing ourselves to acting on our beliefs. With big issues that are rooted in a real life and death struggle, we need to be sure, beyond any doubt, that we can succeed and that our actions are justified, even inevitable.

Economic Satyagraha is also based on the Enlightenment movement's ideas of natural justice. All concepts in Economic Satyagraha and PSP (which will be introduced later) are based on the premise that people are born with a set of human rights that are inextinguishable and non-negotiable throughout their lives.  As humans congregate in a common cause that requires them to submit to the rules of society and law, their inalienable, natural human rights must be maintained, nurtured and protected by society's institutions. If not, the pact of common purpose between the individual and society is broken, null and void.

Satyagraha exponents believe that they can change the world by following simple truth-based principles in their everyday lives. They do this because they sense that we are mindlessly escalating world-wide human rights abuses as well as man-made economic and ecological disasters. To avert future catastrophic events, they discipline their economic actions and willingly make personal sacrifices, especially to stop the build up towards another world war and to alleviate hunger, deaths and poverty.

I believe that world-significant change begins inside the hearts and minds of ordinary people like you and me. We therefore should begin to realise that the world, as it is, can't be changed if we ourselves are unable or unwilling to change first.

Most importantly, Satyagraha devotees are not afraid to publicly dream of a future that values every life and every person's liberty above all other considerations. A future where we no longer demean and befoul our fellow human beings, where we no longer waste and destroy the very basis of our existence;  a future which must intelligently cherish nature's precious gifts in all richness, beauty, diversity and splendor.

It may be becoming clear to you that a Satyagraha is meddling with powerful forces. I am often told that in writing this book I have unleashed a force that will send me to an early grave. So let me be perfectly clear why I am writing this book of peaceful, but dangerous ideas: If we all keep going the way we do "our thing" today, we will all come to a sticky end either through a prolonged war, terrorism, nuclear accidents or simply through the now increasingly prevalent man-made environmental disasters. It is no longer a question of whether we will come to grief, but when. Our already stressed planetary life support and social systems must fail if we go on doing nothing to prevent self-inflicted disasters from happening.

As a wake-up call, let me paint a bleak picture of an unlucky constellation of events which could conceivably happen any day. Imagine the banking system failing again, at the time when the gulf stream stops, creating arctic winters in Europe. Then add conflicts erupting over food scarcities as the world's food bowls, like Australia and then USA and Asia, are gripped by a deep drought. How prepared would the world be to deal with this type of unlucky constellation of natural and man-made events?

*Consider the following paragraph like a TV newsflash interruption...*

*I wrote the above paragraph September 22nd 2009 and awoke on the 23rd to a dust storm in the Blue Mountains near Sydney, Australia. The mornings in the* mountains are usually aglow with a gentle orange red glow. The birds wake us with their noisy calls and their cavorting in the cool of the morning. The mountains are green and the air perfumed with the scent of wildflowers. Today the morning in the mountains is eerily silent. When the usually noisy birds make any sounds at all, they are feeble, scared, timid calls. Nature is in shock. The air is dry, the light a sickly yellow. The mountains, now covered in dust, hold the half-empty drinking water reservoirs of Sydney. Last year, building began on a new drinking water desalination plant in Botany Bay. Harbor ferries are canceled due to poor visibility. The airport has come to a grinding halt and tunnels are shut due to the dust. My wife looked at me in disbelief, then gave me a face mask she bought when the recent swine flu pandemic hit Australia. (Swine flu was thought to have jumped species, because poor farmers were injecting pigs with human growth hormones to stay competitive against the US.) My mother-in-law, now in her eighties, phoned, sounding distressed. She has lived in Sydney all her life and has never seen a dust storm.

My wife just left to drive to work and cautioned me to wear the surgical mask by pointing to the giant, almost one metre long wisteria racemes in our usually lush green garden. They are smothered in a sickly yellow dust, almost thick enough to stop photosynthesis. Welcome to the brave new world of climate change, its political gambles and our careless exploitation and destruction of nature's bounty!

It is spooky to think that I wrote some other passages

*of this book as hurricane Katrina struck New Orleans and the world wondered if this was the beginning of the end for the warm Gulf Stream waters that keep Europe from icing over. We can ignore the problems our economic system causes and stick our heads into the dust. Or we can see these events for what they are: a wake-up call to act more responsibly.*

*The aftermath of this storm was intense. The dust storm reached 2300 meters into the sky and was almost the size of Europe. People were in shock and there was an angry tension in the air – palpable rage over lost opportunities to fix our environmental destruction. Some people even dressed specially for the occasion. I saw one young man on a pedestrian crossing in Springwood. He was in black and wore a tall top hat and a long trench coat. His visible hairline and beard were razor sculptured. His face was stern and solemn. Imagine seeing this foreboding figure striding like death himself. While in the background a yellow-red dust storm rages.*

*The Blue Mountains have always attracted the weird and wacky as well as the three R's. The Rich, the Retired and the Retarded. I live there too. So I guess my mental stability is under suspicion also.*

*The point here is this: the devastation of our natural environment will bring out the worst in us. Be it dressing up in tails and top hat to celebrate judgement day or becoming lawless, regressing into dark anarchic times. Alarm bells are ringing everywhere and, like car alarms going off regularly, the economic and environmental alarm bells have become so*

*commonplace, they are simply ignored. We have become used*
*to the alarms going off at all hours. But are we ignoring the*
*environmental and economic alarms at our own peril?*

-

But, you know, we have alternatives to the doomsday scenario. For example, local councils, big business and our military have the ability, intelligence and the tools to effect positive change. Nobody is better-equipped than town councils, big business and military organisations to act as an agent for change! They command the bulk of our intellectual, natural and economic resources. They should act, if not in the interest of mankind, at least in the interest of their own survival and be protective of their citizens. Admittedly, our institutions will need to be pushed, kicking and screaming, before they change.

A Satyagraha is basically capitalism in reverse. Capitalists, in the traditional- larger than life meaning of the world, make profits by dwarfing and annihilating their opponents. Their profits per sale are, however, extremely small. Corporate grocers, for example, make just one to two percent profit. But because they can dominate or eliminate their competitors, they can multiply this seemingly small profit and end up making billions. This tiny, select class of international shareholder, many of whom are also corporation instead of what our politicians would want us believe – small-scale local investors, simply providing for their pension needs.

In other words, capitalists extract a little from every

one of us. Be it a convenient soft drink, sweets or snack or the steady supply of daily essentials, water, energy, news, entertainment and transport.

A Satyagraha instead deprives undeserving or immoral recipients of their profits simply by refusing to do something. A Satyagraha action is based on a shared mass belief that the corporation is wrong or doing harm. It is a bit like many ants not taking a tiny stick and a tiny bite of food back to their dominant mound, but instead building many small local mounds, depriving the dominant mound of food and materials until it perishes.

The power of one multiplied by a large body of like-minded people, all acting on a shared true and just belief, is a Satyagraha in action! Now, for a moment, indulge your fantasy and imagine that a Satyagraha is pushing for change by withholding purchases – en masse to a corporation. First the Satyagrahy would be ridiculed, then threatened and ultimately, because a corporation consumes massive amount of money, they would cave in when their reserves were used up. Realising the power of a Satyagraha suddenly makes anything and everything possible. We can only argue for change when we are powerful and this power is available to us in a satyagraha.

Churchill lost India to a man dressed in cheese cloth because this seemingly small man was the inventor and commander of the world's most powerful non-violent weapon. What Ghandhi unleashed against the British was a morally strong Satyagraha at work. Gandhi developed Satyagraha from a western as well as eastern ideological foundation which included Russia's Tolstoy, Americas

Thoreau political and economic greats such as Marx, Engel, Henry Ford as well as incorporating India's religious transitions and moral values. Satyagraha, whilst using an amalgamation of Indian terms to describe itself, simply means truth-force. Gandhi's brilliance lies in the fact that he developed Satyagraha as reverse capitalism by valuing individuals' rights above the rights of the community, whilst by contrast the communist and capitalist ideology inflicts and tolerates suffering on individuals for the betterment of society or personal gain.

Gandhi simply beat Churchill's Britain because millions of Indians deprived the British Empire of the profit they needed to suppress and rule India.

Indians en masse disobeyed British directives which generated profits that the British needed to fund the occupation force which suppressed India. No money – no power!

It is ironic when seeing Gandhi standing in a cheese cloth, enduring insults from a beefy Churchill. That old colonial warrior, ruler of the mighty British Empire, was defeated by a simple – *No, we won't buy your products!* Gandhian Satyagraha.

Now consider what unrealised power the internet and other modern forms of communication hold.

Billions of people could be bound in a shared, global belief and suddenly every conceivable change not only appears possible, but has become totally plausible. The only missing ingredient is the will and moral fiber to actually to act!

The Arab spring in 2012 ushered in a long suppressed yearning for human dignity by overthrowing deeply rooted tyrants and again is another example of a Satyagraha – where millions share a belief and achieve massive change.

Other examples are internet-based organisations such as Get-up who have successfully lobbied for many positive changes in Australia.

*The principle of nonviolence dictates the complete abstention from (economic) exploitation of any form.* Gandhi

Wow! Now there is a blast from the past that puts economics and corporate thinking firmly in- the bad boy corner of the rink.

Today's economics in its most debased, popularized form measures human activity and steers and encourages exploitation of the weak informal sector (tech-talk referring to activities which cannot be measured easily, - such as "poor but green and sustainable subsistence farming, small family businesses etc.) . Therefore, instead of helping humanity, most economists simply aid big business by opening access to defenseless markets, where the highest, least risky profits can be obtained. This is done by simply having nigh unlimited resources that enable corporation to outperform, outspend and outwit homegrown enterprises. This distortion of business might frequently create local unemployment and add extra misery to less well educated workers and the middle class of any targeted nation.

Gandhi created non-violent reverse capitalism and reverse or up-side down economics.

Indira Gandhi summed it up thus: "To me, economics is an inseparable part of political freedom...(but) freedom is not freedom... if it does not mean a better deal and more opportunity for the poor and the deprived."

In other words the practice of economics is simply a type of tyranny if it does not serve to lift the lowest from poverty!

In 2011, on a flight to India, I sat besides an economics professor who argued that when a country is economically weak, another better country with an economic advantage could not totally absorb the gain or loss of the weaker country. The argument is better known as the zero sum gain. He was right of course, when you look at statistics using a top down view. Whereas, I argued that when you look at the same picture from the bottom up, having lost opportunities and perhaps one's job to the economically winning country, the same event is felt as a violation – an act of economic brutality that destroys a part of our humanity.

Gandhi's economics are often portrayed as low-brow village idiot sentiments, conjuring up visions of a rural utopian happy worker paradise. This argument is misleading because it is deliberatively dismissive of a man who spent nigh his entire life thinking of ways to lift

India's poor from oppressive poverty. Economists who dismiss Gandhi take the risk of being ridiculed themselves, because when reading Gandhi more deeply one cannot escape the fact that his economic expressions are based on sound economic, empirical observations rather than sentimental clap-trap. The mistake made by high-brows it that they look at Gandhi's simple-minded summary statements, which were penned by his journalistic desire to be a clear, earthy communicator. So instead of giving empirical observations that even today many would find a bit hard-to-digest, he spoke in simple terms, using the language of the people. After all, if Gandhi is knows for anything, then it is for his clarity of purpose and facility in communicating complex ideas to the masses.

*"I must confess that I do not draw a sharp line or any distinction between economics and ethics. Economics that hurt the moral well-being of an individual or a nation are immoral and, therefore, sinful. Thus, the economics that permit one county to prey upon another are immoral."*

Gandhi in this statement sums up Gandhian economics.

If economists were honest, they would endeavor to lift the lowest from poverty and maintain the wealth of hard-working people and nations. But today Gandhian economics are ridiculed to divert attention away from the harm mainstream economists do to the poor and vulnerable. Economics as reported by the media is a mouthpiece of the rich. The unquestioning loyalty practiced by the media is simple immoral – period!

But Gandhi's philosophy of non-violence also states you should not  hate your opponent but attack the argument and not the practitioner or messenger. The point being this: assisting small scale enterprises is generally good for a country, but whilst small airplane components could be made in a 'Ma-and-Pa' factory, an aircraft could not! Therefore, there is room for two types of economic systems the mainstream top-down view of economics and the Gandhian view from the bottom-up which is based on simple respect and love for every human being. Finding enlightenment and deep fulfillment the Gandhian way is to spend one's life in the service to humanity.

I can see a future where a new style economy is running side-by-side with our current aggressive-old-style economy. A dual economic view would also be good for our continued existence on earth. Solving poverty and reducing our aggressive methods of exploitation is good business! It is well known that if poverty were to shrink by a small amount, then big business would receive a humongous windfall. Being flexible and respecting the needs of local communities to economic self-determination and an individual's right to a modest, ennobled life is actually good business. All it takes are a few minor adjustments to current business models.

I personally prefer a fast change to a new economic model. But, most of our fellow citizens in the developed world are relatively content with current arrangements. The lethargy and indifference of the average couch-potato is probably our biggest obstacle to poverty reduction.

Economic Satyagraha books explore and offer vital tools to elevate ourselves to a point where we can become a peaceful force, fully able to change our world into a place which can be enjoyed by all of humanity.

The good professor and I differed on many points and these differences made for interesting conversations that shortened an otherwise long, tedious flight. We both argued our points well and naturally disagreed on most of them. But there was a single point that we agreed on. Namely, that economics is not a hard science but rather a more religious-type-belief that is designed to uphold a widely agreed on value system. Just like our fiat currency is based on the belief that our money has real value, air planes fly because we believe that they can fly...etc... so we know that our fiat money is not backed by gold, but it still doesn't worry us because we have a heavy-duty-religious belief that our economic system is good for us. As long as we hold this belief, nothing will ever change. The rich will grow richer, our planet will face certain ruin and the poor will suffer more and in larger numbers.

Economic Satyagraha could also be used by people who want peace and a reduction in poverty – much like a religion. Some followers would quietly and anonymously play their part in supporting history-making events. Progressive followers would restructure their own communities to raise the living conditions of their fellow citizens. Deeply involved followers would openly challenge and debate economic wrongdoers and take them to task, demanding justice for the oppressed.

Without a doubt, Economic Satyagraha believers

would contribute to the building of a world based on our deeply-rooted childhood desires of natural justice and world peace.

The link between morality, spirituality and economics is not a thin tenuous thread that is easily broken. It is a strong integral part of us. Indian spirituality is much clearer about the workings and strength of this link than western spirituality. However, they are identical in nature and have the same effect and worth. The differences are just superficial expressions and methods of practicing spirituality.

Let me use Gandhi as an example. When he said he loves humanity, he had developed and practiced the willpower to think this in his mind, and felt in his heart that he loved humanity before the words were spoken by his mouth. There was no distinction between what he thought and what he said. Therein lies the strength of Satyagraha as a force for truth. Gandhi's mind lifted every individual human being to the level of God –a true miracle of creation that holds the divine powers of self-awareness, love and willpower. He ascribed these powers to every human being and believed that every human being holds them with equal strength. However, these powers need to be unlocked and developed with the aid of a guide, guru, religious leader or simply by learning from the love practiced by good people.

But how does this divine love force connect to economics? Gandhi believed that if there is a disconnect between thought – which is a love-feeling for what is right – and our actions, then this disconnect creates unhappiness and stress. Whereas, when we do "the right thing" our thought are at ease and our actions flow gently with ease, creating a sense of calm and happiness within us as well as externally through our actions.

So, to just for a moment put the boot into phrases such as "it's just business" and the stock market's "greed is good" credo – these are, in Gandhi's eyes, just means of aggression that create unhappiness and misery, stress and strife both personally and for humanity at large.

When we view economics as a Gandhian force for love and peace, then we realise that we as individuals hold the key to world peace and happiness and that, when we act collectively as a religious-like truth force, we already possess the right weapon to change the world for the better. Gandhi opened the spiritual door to economics for both east and west, because he demonstrated on a grand scale that individual moral actions can defeat even the mightiest empire. Churchill's British Empire was ultimately defeated by the power of one. Gandhi's brilliance lies in the fact that he took the theory of non-violence and demonstrated to the world on a grand scale, how to do it.

Today, two billion plus people are connected via the internet and acting together as a moral force has become very easy. It is obvious that the time for peaceful change lies in the here and now, because the balance of power has shifted in favor the masses and away from the controls of government and corporations.

But when looking at communication revolutions such as the Arab spring uprisings against their dictators in 2011 and Julian Assange's WikiLeaks opening the Pandora's box of political double-talk, we realise the fragility of our communication technologies. The Arabs had mobile phone technology used against them by their government while Assange has his funding frozen. We can already see in 2011 that free internet communication and phone communication technologies are beginning to be shut down by court actions, dictatorial governments and corporate filtering of information flow. Technology keys are turned on and off by corporations and banks which have usually no scruples taking money from illicit operators, but are happy to cut funding to Wikileaks by blocking internet processed donations.

In humanity's epic journey through the ages, we have left many beliefs behind us. The earth is no longer flat and we can divide the formerly indivisible atom. It is time that humanity's misplaced trust in traditional forms of leadership, trust, representative government, economics, trade, war and peace are re-examined and much of what is accepted today as inevitable, is left behind, as relics from a darker time. With luck, we might even learn to measure our worth against the simple truths of natural justice, which is shown by how we treat the lowliest human being in our daily encounters. Peace, love and truth are deeply embedded in our hearts and only a strong moral force can subdue our destructive urges.

# *Who will throw the first stone?*

---

**For Gandhi,** the roots of violence lie in:

*"Wealth without work, pleasure without conscience, knowledge without character, commerce without morality, science without humanity, worship without sacrifice, politics without principles."*

I am borrowing here from Gandhi and paraphrase him when I state that: *We, the rich and educated, have no right to eat drink and be merry until the poor are clothed and fed!*

Why, may you ask, do I, as a writer, not shun pinching ideas from Gandhi? The answer is simple: Gandhi gave humanity a valuable gift...

Mohandas Karamchand Gandhi

October 2, 1869 - January 30, 1948

Lawyer, founder of non-violent Satyagraha, civil rights activist, anti-apartheid activist, economist, moralist, holy man (Mahatma, title and practice which he hated), humanist and father of modern India where he is revered as *Man of the Century*.

Satyagraha is a non-violent ideology invented and practiced by Gandhi. He adapted it from ancient Indian and more modern day American and Russian disobedience philosophies.

He was deeply influenced by America's Thoreau Russia's Tolstoy and India's many ancient religions as well as Christianity. His life's work was identifying and amplifying what all these teachings have in common and coining the phrase and philosophy Satyagraha - or truth force. Satyagraha's communality chose a solid foundation at the heart of humanity and ignored wealth, language, color and gender.

During his lifetime he shaped, reshaped and practiced non-violent Satyagraha into a perfect truth that can still withstand and challenge the power of government. *Economic* Satyagraha takes over where Gandhi left off by tapping into a planet-wide awakening of the forces which create and maintain poverty. But it must be understood that Gandhi made no distinction between economics, ethics and truth. In his teachings, he describes economics only as a tool that must help ordinary people to have a better life, instead of a tool which just helps the rich to become richer…which, sadly, is the dominating current form of economic thinking. He viewed economics that worsen human misery as an act of war like aggression. Because he linked economics to moral acts, he has been ridiculed by greed based economists as a simplistic peasant idyll economist. Whilst main stream economists try hard to silence, ignore and sideline him, they still use his moral economic teachings to justify themselves by publishing distorted economic statistical scales. Typically, they would argue that millions in a county will benefit hugly from cheaper books, if only the local book industry, which only employs a few thousand people, would have all  protection removed, opening it up to free market forces. For Gandhi the suffering of the few thousand would have been an intolerable price to pay because such economic nonsense only know the price of objects and not their full cultural and humanistic value.

Gandhi created and first used something like a Satyagraha philosophy to morally uplift its followers into a non-violent struggle against South Africa's apartheid and later, when Satyagraha was fully developed, turned it into a non-violent weapon/force against India's colonial oppressors. It must be clearly understood that he likened non-violence to a weapon and not some airy-fairy notion of passive hippie submissiveness.

Gandhi is quoted as having said:

*"Love does not burn others, it burns itself. Therefore, a Satyagrahi, i.e., a civil resister, will joyfully suffer even unto death.*

*It follows, therefore, that a civil resister, whilst he will strain every nerve to compass the end of the existing rule, will do no intentional injury in thought, word or deed to the person of a single* [oppressor]."

I would sum up his non violence ideology thus: *Non violence is a hard path to follow and not for the week and best avoided by the cowardly.*

Historically, Satyagraha followers who came from India's indigenous religious beliefs practiced self-effacement, humility, patience and faith. Fasting is today still seen as a powerful tool to achieve personal self-restraint which is used to outwardly show determination and courage.

In 2011, Anna Hazare, an Indian modern day

Gandhian politician, has succeeded in forcing India's government to enact a Lokpal bill that will eventually fight big-boy corruption by sitting above the parliament. He basically began a fast to death and would not stop unless the bill was passed by parliament. He is daily headline new in India and his antics caught the world's attention on many occasions. Naturally, he is put under intense scrutiny and his party was not as pure as he hoped, but he skillfully turned this into another crusade – planning for a new party constitution which would end the blemished practices. As a comic relief, he also took a vow of silence for a few weeks when the media blowtorch was turned on his own party, thus avoiding awkward probing questions from the press with an muffled *hmmm* or using a skilled press speaker as a proxy. He is a true Gandhian politician, holding a national government to ransom and being a modern-day, slippery, media-savvy politician at the same time.

Gandhi insisted that Satyagraha practitioners must strictly follow society's laws, but that they should reserve the personal right to practice civil disobedience when laws contravene natural justice (especially human rights).

I believe that every human being has the inalienable right to practice a Satyagraha of their own. I have personally begun to test my actions against Satyagraha ideas and have coined the modern expression Economic Satyagraha. Additionally, I especially reserve the right to practice economic non-compliance when economics is used as a covert form of violence. I also believe that anyone has the right to practice Economic Satyagraha covertly or overtly, because it is ultimately a belief system and as Goethe said "Die Gedanken sind frei..." [Thoughts are free]

You don't need anyone's permission to be moral and to appropriate some standards of behavior and wisdom from Satyagraha.

Just help yourself to be morally and spiritually uplifted. After all, Satyagraha is a gift given to all of humanity, and using it, like breathing, is our birthright.

But we all need a limbo bar that can set a demarcation line, to guide our conscience. Limbo dance below it and you are free of moral guilt or jump it, taking the easy option and you are enslaved in amorality. Satyagraha will do that, but life, and the world around us, is complicated and I know from bitter personal experience that an ideal Economic Satyagraha cannot exist, and that I frequently have to compromise my ideals to survive in my environment. But there are many instances where I do have the power to act and I can quickly and clearly distinguish good from bad and am making more and more good economically non-violent choices.

Appropriating some Satyagraha ideas does not involve a rock hard destination, but rather an ongoing journey through life that increasingly more clearly distinguishes between violence and the non-violent action we perform in our daily lives. It is an acquired taste, that once discovered becomes addictive and compulsive in the most pleasant way imaginable. A Satyagraha based morality basically offers Satyagraha followers a superior moral and intellectual foundation and is a powerful truth that supports our personal opposition to unjust laws and unjust economic actions.

Perhaps, like Anna Hazare, some Gandhian followers will don the white, 50s inspired ice cream vendor's hat and white kaftan and become politicians after having given away all their earthly wealth, living only off the goodwill they earn from the people they represent in their political truth-based actions. But for the moment these people are confined to India. But, who know, you might just be the right person to do it in your country using your own dress mode. Like him or loath him, Julian Assange kind of did it, giving away his wealth and living off the goodwill of supporters, but he found himself in too many beds, embraced too many followers and is now suffering the consequences of his moral lapses. These character weaknesses ultimately gave his enemies the tools to destroy him.

Gandhi warned about the disconnect of mind and matter and tried all kinds of cleansing rituals to purify his mind and actions. But he has always been an impossibly hard act to follow and Julian was just human when giving in to a plethora of temptation traps. The next person who wants to try being a public Satyagrahi saint should study Gandhi and remember that it is easy for our morals to jump the limbo bar that Gandhi set, but that it is tough to limbo under it and set yourself morally free.

Satyagraha is based on three fundamental ideals: satya meaning truth, implying openness, honesty, and fairness. Ahimsa, meaning physical and mental non-violence; and tapasya, literally referring to self-sacrifice to obtain truth and justice.

In Gandhi's words:

*"In the application of Satyagraha, I discovered, in the earliest stages, that pursuit of Truth did not admit violence being inflicted on one's opponent, but that [they] must be weaned from error by patience and sympathy. For, what appears to be truth to the one, may appear to be an error to the other. And patience means self-suffering. So (Satyagraha) became to mean vindication of Truth, not by infliction of suffering on the opponent, but [by inflicting suffering] on one's own self."*

Gandhi realised that non-violence requires incredible faith and courage, which not everyone possessed. He therefore advised that everyone need not keep to non-violence, especially if it was used as a cover for cowardice. Gandhi guarded against attracting to his Satyagraha movement those who feared to take up arms or felt themselves incapable of resistance. He did not want cowards in his movement. Nor did he want to attract those who though Indians was justified in fighting the British Raj with vengeful violence.

*"I do believe that where there is only a choice between cowardice and violence, I would advise violence."* Ghandi sought to clearly separate the violent from the peaceful struggle.

To paraphrase Gandhi: *in non-violence Satyagraha followers come into possession of a force infinitely superior to the one they had before. But if they do not* adhere to non-violence, then they should have nothing to do with non-violence and resume the arms they possessed before. Because their bravery consisted not in being good marksmen but in defying death and being ever ready to bare their breasts to the bullets.

"The essence of non-violent resistance is that it seeks to eliminate antagonisms without harming the antagonists themselves, as opposed to violent resistance, which is meant to cause harm to the antagonist. A Satyagrahi therefore does not seek to end or destroy the relationship with the antagonist, but instead seeks to transform or "purify" it to a higher level."

A better known term used for Satyagraha is that it is a "silent force" or a "soul force" (a term also used by Martin Luther King Jr. during his famous "I Have a Dream" speech). It arms the individual with moral power rather than physical power. Satyagraha is also termed a "universal force", as it essentially "makes no distinction between kinsmen and strangers, young and old, man and woman, friend and foe."

"I have drawn the distinction between passive resistance as understood and practised in the West and Satyagraha before I had evolved the doctrine of the latter to its full logical and spiritual extent.

I often used 'passive resistance' and 'Satyagraha' as synonymous terms: but as the doctrine of Satyagraha developed, the expression 'passive resistance' ceases even to be synonymous, as passive resistance has admitted violence as in the case of suffragettes and has been *universally acknowledged to be a weapon of the weak.*

*Moreover passive resistance does not necessarily involve complete adherence to truth under every circumstance. Therefore it is different from Satyagraha in three essentials:*

*Satyagraha is a weapon of the strong; it admits of no violence under any circumstance whatever; and it ever insists upon truth.*

*I think I have now made the distinction perfectly clear."*

Mohandas Karamchand Gandhi,

While writing this book I discovered many unpleasant truths and wondered at times if only a bloody revolution could restore some sanity into our current economic and conventional wars. I disturbingly observed that many call for an eye-for-an-eye, but to paraphrase Gandhi: *"An eye for an eye only leads to blind hate,"* and blind hate and greed has led us to the edge of atomic extinction as the atomic doomsday clock after 2011, is now closer to atomic midnight as it was during the cold war.

# *Non violence is not for cowards!*

---

If we want to take the *"profit out of poverty"* (Martin Luther King jnr.), then we must be prepared for personal sacrifices because we are personally both the cause and the solution to the problem. Economic Satyagraha proposes taking personal responsibility for our independent local economies and requires civil disobedience and economic non-compliance. We have to show local restraint to obtain global justice!

The spinning wheel in the Indian congress flag reminds us that colonialism was broken by weaving and wearing locally made clothing that deprived the English oppressors of their profits. Economic issues should not be regarded as boring or unimportant; they are bloody-minded ideologies which lead to deprivation, conflict and death.

We must realise that our daily purchase decisions affect the well-being of the entire world's human population. Our greed or abstinence from unjust profits and our over-consumption will dictate if people elsewhere live, die or endure appalling conditions.

Modern day Economic Satyagraha action can be as simple as:-

> Global accountability and local responsibility
> for planetary problems.

Global truths and natural justice.

Ethical, civic-friendly local taxation.

Self-sufficient local economies.

Responsible trade based on an exchange of real values.

Power sharing through PSP.

Living green by rebuilding our wasteful cities.

Ethical shopping.

Decentralised small scale manufacturing using 3d print technologies.

I hope that I have not scared you too much with the ideals of Satyagraha. But we need to be reminded that even peaceful disobedience has serious repercussions and that we need to be prepared to answer for our actions – even if it is only to ourselves and our sense of morality and righteousness.

Reignited by the rise and fall of Nazi Germany, people have asked the question: *Are good people bad when they stand by and do nothing?*

We are today more than ever confronted with the age-old dilemma of being either condemned for doing nothing or being condemned as activists and trouble makers. If this book does nothing other than answer the vital question of whether it is better to act on our beliefs when discovering injustices or to do nothing and be judged as accomplices to economic atrocities then it has succeeded in creating a moral compass in you.

The main point is this. In Hitler's day, good people were not as well informed and much too obedient to oppose authority, so o they had, at least in the early days of Hitler's reign of terror, some justification to excuse themselves for not acting and for not protecting innocent lives. But today we have the power of one, are very well educated and well informed. Our excuses for not acting in a just humane manner are wearing thin.

# *Divine mercy: a spiritual alternative to violence*

---

I came across a heart-wrenching story at the crossroads of a bloody conflict, which should have ended with the spilling of more blood, but did not. Instead it is an uplifting tale of the human spirit that shows a clear alternative to violence. The meaning of this story is hidden behind religious philosophical language which makes it hard to understand at first glance.

I am myself an agnostic, an undecided fence-sitter who neither believes in God nor disbelieves in God. I neither judge religions and religious devotion, nor do I believe the atheist's mantra that life on earth was an accident – that there is no magic, no wonder, no higher power or any law of nature that, with a God-like purpose, created life on earth. Likewise, the concept of heaven and hell is not alien to me, but I see them instead as self-evident opposites representing a powerful picture of misery and peace of mind.

Looking at this story, with this blank, open mind, I found a deep human truth in a religiously-inspired tale of unconditional love. It is best told by Narda Azaria Dalgleish herself. I have, however, allowed myself the liberty of condensing her message here in order to clarify her main point to make it accessible:

*In early October 2004... my son, Rotem Moria, was blown-up by Al-Qaeda in Sinai... By a supernatural act of grace at the moment of hearing the news ...I was spared of any reaction of hate, anger, vengeance or blame... I was engulfed at once by a presence of Love ... misguided though they may be... In the midst of terror...Love stripped away the illusion of the polarity ...and united ...in the vision that it, itself, is the single indivisible Identity of all things and all people, including that of a son, his murderer and their mothers"*

We had connected by chance on the *wiserearth.org* website and had this conversation.

She wrote: *"the very strong/bold Economic Satyagraha link which has the quote - "He who is not angry when there is just cause for anger is immoral. Why? Because anger looks to the good of justice. And if you can live amid injustice without anger, you are immoral as well as unjust." Aquinas, 1225-1274. Perhaps another, subtle, way of looking at it, as suggested by the great contemporary of Aquinas, Ibn Arabi, who saw the state of anger as an inability to receive Divine Mercy..."*

I replied:- "*I agree ! Just from a slightly different point of view. Anger stems from an inability to experience or bring about a state of Divinity or Divine Mercy (which is clearly visible and totally comprehensible, to the angry person, but cannot be reached without a struggle). Therefore, anger is a motivator to overcome disappointment and a sense of powerlessness. Anger is an absence of equilibrium between what is and what could or should be.*"

Narda turned rage and hate into love and a desire to do good. No one would blame her if she had expressed her feelings in terms of a "justifiable hunger for revenge". But she saw beyond "an eye for an eye" and looked beyond the war into the hearts of the killers and into the hearts of the killers' mothers. She saw the yearning for a state of divinity and the killing of her son as an act that occurred when *"righteous anger"* deviated from a righteous struggle for a love of divinity and turned instead to murder, hate and war.

Divine Mercy is a strange antiquated concept to the modern west that is rarely discussed or understood in the developed world. So permit me to put a modern spin on it and say that Divine is simply a religious term which describes an act of God. For me it describes something which is not under our control, but instead is entirely controlled by a supernatural being. Whereas, in an act of mercy, I conjure up images of lying prostrate hoping to be mercifully spared.

In my opinion, Divine Mercy is more like saying "End hunger and poverty in our life time." or like wishing for world peace. I think of Divine Mercy simply as a mental state of mind which we can conceive as being so "real" that, given the right conditions, it could actually come into existence!

For example: We can easily imagine a world free from hunger, disease and war. But we have no idea of how to get there and feel an inner anger and rage when this ideal is threatened or ridiculed. Likewise, we feel elated when we get a little closer to solving these overwhelming and intractable problems.

I got to understand Narda's ideology during our exchanges and realised that when she talks of Divine Mercy, she describes a world free from war, hunger, poverty and disease, a world free of hate and avarice. She can conceive such a world, and clearly sees how this world would function. She can imagine meeting her son's killers face to face without feeling hate, because, in her mind, the future dream has already become a reality. Narda chooses to look past the blood and hate that surrounds her currently, and instead sees people as if they had already arrived and were already living in a world free from hunger, disease, poverty, war and hate. She treats her enemies in her daily encounters as if they were meeting in paradise – in the state of Divine Mercy.

To illuminate this point, imagine a soldier targeting an enemy in his gun sight. The point at which the soldier decides to shoot and continues his struggle through war, and the suicide bomber decides to detonate the bomb, thinking of heaven, is where Narda instead imagines she is in the state of Divine Mercy. She feels love and compassion that her enemies at this point in time do not deserve. She imagines a point after the war and acts on this image with love and respect for life.

Confronted with the same situation, a soldier is primed and ready to kill for a peaceful and better future world, while a suicide bomber detonates a bomb, thinking of their place in heaven, wasting their lives and destroying countless others for a utopian struggle which upends logic for a peaceful, better world…in their own ideological framework, which differs only slightly from that of the soldier with the gun.

. They confuse their despicable acts with a ticket to paradise, whereas their actions actually have earned them a ticket to hell because they have condemned their victims to a man-made hell on earth.

By contrast, Narda's enlightened state of mind is the foundation of a truly peaceful struggle for a righteous cause. She looks past the carnage to live and act as if she is already living in a future where divine mercy is the norm not the exception. Thus, she performs an act of divine mercy- by not retaliating against her sons killing and by placing herself mentally at a peaceful point in the future – thus quieting and stilling the current pain and anger.

It is a bit like turning the other cheek only more dangerous to the practitioner but profoundly deep, and for most of us who live in a narcissistic oriented society almost totally inaccessible and incomprehensible.

Another example of divine mercy can be found in Gandhi's Satyagraha movement. But instead of being purely spiritual, Gandhi's example is a hands-on, action-filled form of divine mercy.

Gandhi's Satyagraha movement was one of the biggest non-violent peace movements the world has ever witnessed. But even a peaceful Satyagraha can easily unleash the hell-hounds of war. Gandhi himself used his power as a revered living God and threatened opponents and followers alike that he would kill himself through fasting, in order to maintain peace between opponents. The British knew that, should he die whist imprisoned, civil war was inevitable. Nevertheless, his followers were equally threatened that he, a living God, would rather die than watch them commit acts of violence and bloody murder.

The salient point is that Gandhi treated his opponents as if they already all lived happily in paradise. His opponents' violence therefore did not matter or warrant a violent response. Instead, he demonstrated that calm acceptance of violence and stubborn disobedience were a more powerful tool in his "cold war" against the British Raj. He behaved as if he walked in paradise, which is why many spiritual people recognised him as a living God. But far from being purely spiritual he relished every chance to convert his enemies to his point of view.

A modern interpretation of Satyagraha must therefore be firmly based in non-violence and a love for our opponents. A Satyagraha is an epic struggle and every bit as powerful as any weapon of war. Even though it is a peaceful struggle it is not for cowards. It requires a steely determination and an unshakable moral position.

Gandhi realised that power comes in two forms: as raw economic power that fuels greed and wars and as a moral inner strength which can prevent the accumulation of power in the hands of tyrannic rulers. For example, Australia went to war against terrorists, without a United Nations mandate and against the opposition of some of the largest peace time rallies since the Vietnam war. Peace-loving Australians simply lacked the power and organisational skills to veto the decisions of their democratically-elected rulers. With the power of hindsight and new insights into Gandhi's economics, I now know that we could have stopped Australia from entering this war by organising an anti war Satyagraha.

Gandhi realised that the inner strength of India was a more powerful tool than the military and economic strength of India's oppressors. Gandhi figured that this power came from the engine of commerce; ie., from the seemingly mundane things we put into our shopping trolleys – the foods we eat, the clothing we wear and the energy we consume. To describe this peaceful weapon of change, I coined the phrase *Economic Satyagraha* which is the topic of a series of book on interrelated topics.

Let us seek to find a moral position that can serve in an epic struggle to end poverty, war, diseases and hunger for all times, a position which gives us the right, power and moral authority to complain on behalf of the hungry and dispossessed masses.

# *Liberal economic politics – a new type of slavery*

It is easy to ramble on about how bad the world is and how we are on the edge of a crevasse which will swallow us whole unless we seek salvation in carbon credits.

Have you ever wondered why carbon trading alone holds the only salvation for humanity's environmental destructiveness? What is so special about a tax that lets the public carry the burden while the polluters are given huge amounts of money, which immediately adds to their profits, so they can keep on polluting as if nothing has changed? I must be dumb, because try as I may, I can't understand this logic.

Why is this Carbon Tax so confusing to us? What should we believe?

Let's me try to sort out what is propaganda and what constitutes just idealist wishful thinking.

Say some big-wig corporation makes steel in Wollongong, a sea-side pearl of a town in New South Wales, Australia. The Gong, as the locals call it, meanders along a picturesque strip of narrow coastline, seemingly forever wedged between high coal laden cliffs and the roaring Pacific Ocean. The town stretches from one horizon to the other, panoramically picture-perfect as an endless string of sandy beaches and inviting bays, without exaggeration, for as far as the eye can see. Oh, did I mention the blooming big steelwork belching soot from an endless variety of infernal smoke stacks 24/7, right at the heart of the Gong, voted in 2010 Australia's cleanest beach – go figure! Port Kembla?

What is a steel corporation to do with a looming carbon offset tax? Taking the money and running is a good option, which is exactly what they are doing over the next few years. Downsizing has already begun whilst shifting their steel making into counties where the sovereign risk (which is in plain English: government interference in profit-earning potential) is very low as long as the bribes are high and paid on time.

Call me a cynic, but when a quick back of an envelope calculation shows that just one year of carbon tax money would replace 20% of Australia's household electricity consumption with wind/solar/wave power, creating countless secure green jobs in green manufacturing, construction and maintenance of green power infrastructure, how could anyone take the carbon tax seriously?

Mainstream economics is all about securing corporate incomes and making investing in these corporations easy for the super-wealthy. In 2011, I spent some time in India, setting up 3dStuffmaker, a 3d printing open source printer maker that uses a technology which will herald the next Industrial Revolution by putting a high-tech factory on every desk-top, killing many of today's giant manufacturing plants with stuff made/replicated at home.

While there, I spent many boring nights watching Indian TV, which consists mostly of watching gyrating wobbling bobbling Bollywood or seriously devoted religious broadcasting. I frequently flipped and hit the remote after experiencing an overload of dancing, singing, tabla tapping, family tie shows and seriously devoted praying – ending up all too often at the local version of business news.

Indian business TV, for the uninitiated, is gruesomely honest and refreshingly down to earth. A company doesn't just experience tight cash-flow. Their directors are interviewed red-faced and asked openly: "When do you think, sir, your company is actually going broke and closing down?"

I quickly learned how brutal economics actually is when we remove whitewashing western acronyms from distasteful corporate actions.

In summary, commentators reasoned that it is difficult to invest in India because the country has too many small and micro-sized businesses that makes it too difficult for corporations to compete. This then causes a lack of A grade stock market listings, which in turn makes it difficult for large scale investors to find a safe haven for their money in India. As a remedy, commentators frequently suggest opening up the Indian market further by removing government petrol price fixing and retail protection for small traders. Additionally, it is suggested that India must invest in more large-scale, super-big, privatized, infrastructure projects, which then would attract more foreign investors, allowing them to harvest profits from essential consumption. This is eco-babble-talk for tapping into the locals' essentials like water, food, energy and transport, effectively white-anting the locals and sending the profits overseas.

This is good, right? Because it grows India's economy!

Wrong. *The Hindu*, Thursday Nov 10, 2011, editorial reads thus: "The Human Development Report 2011 of the UNDP affirms what critical scholars have been saying for years now: the high economic growth achieved by India has not translated into a better quality of life for the vast majority of its citizens." Period! High economic growth means less basic human prosperity for the poor.

The editorial continues "… economist Jean Dreze and Nobel laureate Amartya Sen highlight destructive aspects of India's (economic) growth, such as the razing of forests, indiscriminate mining, the drying of rivers, and the massacre of fauna. This thoughtless (economic) cause has invited a strong public backlash in some places as vulnerable communities feel the effects."

It concludes: "Soil erosion, water stress desertification and deforestation is expected to continue. These factors are likely to intensify climate change, with impoverishing consequences."

So much for the zero sum argument the kindly professor I met on my flight to India believed in. Indian economic commentators have a much clearer view of economics from the bottom up than our top down economic viewpoint. India is a bit like an ant looking up and realizing its vulnerability.

The evidence is mounting to suggest that economic growth creates and deepens poverty. India's economy grew in 2010 and 2011 by about 7.5% while the purchasing power of the poor was reduced by up to 30%. So, even if we buy into the argument that economic growth raises poor household incomes by a little less than the economic growth of their nation, the poor still lost 20% in real value. That means 20% less food and essentials for over 40% of the world's poor who reside in

India. Yet India is held up by leading economists as one of the world's wonder economies. Well one has to conclude that someone is telling porkies and it surely ain't the starving, infant mortality-grieving, illiterate, short life expectancy-afflicted, voiceless poor!

Ajay Chhibber, Assistant Secretary General UN and regional director –Asia Pacific, UNDP wrote in the *Economic Times Chennay* 19 Nov 2011, in an article on inclusive sustainable growth, "...growth has been increasingly jobless, (while) employment has declined..." In plain speak, this means that, whilst India's economy has grown, no new jobs were added and unemployment has deepened as corporate efficiencies in automation ruthlessly reduces hand labour. He concluded: "As we gobble up the world's resources, rising oil and food prices are estimated to have caused a drop in purchasing power of the 20% of the population by a quarter." He closes with a Gandhian quote: "The world has enough to meet everyone's need but not enough for everyone's greed."

I basically believe the UNDP's evidence and add that, in my opinion, poverty exists because we use an aggressive profit extraction-based economic system (law of rent). After years researching Economic Satyagraha, I've come to the conclusion that poverty exists because we entrust our affairs to remote leaders, because we lack a power-sharing system like PSP, and because anyone who enjoys First World standards is quietly profiting from the maintenance of perpetual poverty and war.

Where did I find the evidence to justify my beliefs? The answer lies in my research methods, that long before I discovered Gandhi's Satyagraha, were already developing truths or base lines. A truth or baseline is constructed over time by testing, say, a politician's policy against a truth that is rooted in reality. Like killing, or cutting some one's life short, is illegal as well as morally apprehensive. I simply look at a policy statement from two or more extreme ends of opposing points of view.

The UNDP measurement indicates that, when GDP grows in India, the poorest in Indian suffer. The richest Indians, however, grow richer. So I can begin to claim that it is probably true to say "that the rich grow richer *because* the poor grow poorer." It is even more likely to be a truth when viewed by the poorest Indian's perspective. Looking up at the rich and it is a stronger truth again when the richest Indian is looking down their noses, confirm it as well. It is an irrefutable truth, that when the life expectancy of the poor is shortening and that of the rich extended. As evidence builds up, a truth invariably comes up with the same answers, whereas a falsehood only looks good in the mouths of spin doctors. If I slowly poison millions of people, shortening their lives by years, for financial gain, I must expect to be punished. But if I can do it economically and be a hero in the financial tabloids, then it is true to say that this injustice *still* deserves severe punishment because it kills millions before their time! That simple, testable truth was Gandhi's truth. If economics hurt people, then it is a form of greed-based aggression that deserves our contempt.

That's the bad news. The good news is that I believe poverty and wars are consumption-driven juggernauts, that our monetary system is based on the illusion that money can be stored in infinite volumes, even though it is not backed by anything other than our fervent believe in its existence (Fiat currency). It's a bit like hope based on the hope that hope is real.

This raises the following questions:

- What is money?

- Where does it come from?

- Where is proof that it exists?

- Why should we believe in its existence?

Factually, our money is not backed by gold or infrastructure or anything tangible. It is technically called a fiat currency. Fiat is a Latin-derived word meaning "let it be done" or known on my behalf/behest. Today it means a government-backed decree, promising that its money is real, as in the word *tangible*. But instead it is clearly intangible as in the word *illusion*. It is actually backed by our consumption of everyday things like water, food and the purchase of branded consumer goods. This consumption is channelled through political and big business monopolies, which are designed to exclude the world's poor from participating in the necessities and joys of life.

The easiest way to build wealth is to get a small amount every time people use necessities like water, housing, transport, food. The wealth created by essential consumption is so large that governments used to fund large portions of their national budgets from essential consumption profits. Cheap public transport was subsidised by rail freight. Roads were build and maintained by petrol users though hidden taxes. Banks and airlines paid into pension funds and luxury foods subsidised the essentials. Now under user-pay policies and private-public partnerships, rich and poor alike pay. Whilst the rich can easily afford to pay, the poor gradually slip back, barely being able to afford essentials; this condemns millions to languish on a hand-to-mouth treadmill. It is a classic case of corporations internalising profits derived from the public for the benefit of the already rich and externalising costs to be paid by the state or consumer. This phenomenon can be observed in rich countries like Australia where people have, after years on the hand-to-mouth welfare treadmill, become a new class of institutionalised poor. It is also apparent in countries like India – except there an iron faith that God will provide, keeps the poor sane and somewhat tame. But extra stress due to corruption, caste and poor education is taking its toll and sporadic violence erupts easily among the poor. I met a packaging salesman with his arm in plaster. He had it broken with an iron bar after a minor car accident. What in the west is a nuisance incident turns into a full blown riot when the poor person's property or person is damaged or injured even accidentally. Whilst the percentage of poor people is statistically falling in counties like India, the margin that keeps them out of poverty is wafer thin and any setback is deeply felt.

It is therefore most unsettling to realise that we as consumers drive the engine of poverty. We are the direct beneficiaries of the profits which are denied to the working poor in our own countries and the poor, powerless and dispossessed of our planet.

We are the foot soldiers, the mindless *Mitläufer* (blind followers) who choose to look the other way, partially because it is painful to admit, and partially because our society hides and whitewashes the proceeds of our blood-stained complicity.

The good news is that this situation can be changed quickly. This change can be violent or happen slowly and peacefully, giving everyone time to adjust. Economic Satyagraha demonstrates, debates and describes the forces, and offers hope that a change that bonds rich and poor in a tango to the death, can start to be turned down to a more equitable relationship. This process can be relatively peaceful within the legal confines of our system and be at peace with our personal morals.

I liken an Economic Satyagraha to the abolition of slavery. In its beginnings, few people thought ill of slavery. In the end, through a civil war and finally through an act of parliament, it was condemned as morally corrupt. Today, we see slavery as abhorrent, but we must not forget that it took two hundred long years of struggle to establish the moral superiority of anti-slavery campaigners. I think that we are at the beginning of the two-hundred-year-long moral struggle to abolish poverty. I even go so far as claiming that the public at large has no understanding of how poverty, war and hunger are created. Nor do most First World people see anything wrong with the way they live. I don't think for a moment that the vast majority understands the connection between their First World life style and poverty.

Even I have no complaints about our economy's workings in regard to my own wellbeing. But, I am a moral person who agonises over rights and wrongs. I also have eyes and the power of reasoning, which my mind's eye uses to cast a very pervasive, long and dark shadow on the achievements of our civilisation. I can see an unavoidable dark end of our current world order, its glory and its killings. I can't get myself to rejoice in our achievement while our most basic morals are dragging in the gutter of poverty, hunger, war and injustice.

How can we celebrate, when our outdated economic and political system exploits 80% of the world's population, in order to sustain our First World, fairytale life-style?

I dream of a future when Economic Satyagraha followers will be seen as visionaries who could envisage a better future and who laid plans to usher it in. In the meantime, we flounder in a mixture of confused beliefs. But I hope that like the first anti-slavery campaigners, we will find a strength that separates us from irrational dreamers and lunatics. I have tried to develop Economic Satyagraha as a tool that helps anti-war, anti-poverty and natural justice campaigners to define and defend our position.

I sent an early version of this book to Ela Gandhi, the granddaughter of Gandhi. She understood the issue immediately and put her finger right on it when she said: "*Both Martin Luther King and Gandhiji were able to mobilise millions of people. Can we?*" ... and this is the salient point about a Satyagraha. The hardest part about starting an Economic Satyagraha is not only to fire people's imagination and to stir their conscience or to rally them to the cause. The hardest issue is to have people accept that our economic system is a problem at all. We are conditioned to think that poverty happens because people live in dictatorships and are suffering under a corrupt regime.

An article about a Mumbai-held Democratic Capitalism forum was reporting in Chennai's *New Indian Express* 15/11/11, as India "has to generate jobs for the millions of young Indians joining the workforce every year..." Even senior economists threw their weight behind a new "manufacturing for livelihood" policy that must deliver at least 100 million new jobs. Manufacturing for livelihood means not just more jobs for young Indians in large export-oriented factories, but also new competition to large-scale manufacturing from hi-tech table-top manufacturing plant. The small number of well-capitalised and super-efficient enterprises around the world will therefore feel the heat of millions of livelihood-creating mum-and-dad skilled manufacturing, value-adding enterprises.

The proof of why it will happen lay in the conclusion of an associated article where it was claimed that "there has been innovation to develop products aligned to the needs of the bottom of the pyramid" and a call on government to explore "...the use of technology for the benefit of the people."

Coming from economists and capitalist leaders, these statements sounds more like Communist rhetoric than captain of industry dictates. Strangely, Gandhi's economic ideas, long lampooned as village idylls, are getting legs in the real world, sixty to seventy-odd years after he formulated and refined them. Gandhi was a deep thinker who based his assumption on tested truths. He was able to oust the British from India, using nothing other than millions of spinning wheels – technology that dates back to the dawn of humankind. But he knew its power, because his reasoning was based on infallible logic and tested truths!

It is an inevitability, using Gandhi's logic, that the next industrial revolution will happen on table-tops in our neighbourhoods. The economic power generated by millions of mums and dads beavering away to make hi-tech, high value stuff, will have severe repercussions around the world as mega-manufacturers falter, forever readjusting the balance of power from centralised dictatorships to decentralised neighbourhood economics. Nation after nation will have to regain their economic and power distribution as millions will turn to table top manufacturing for their daily bread.

Most of us would  never make a connection between our personal conduct and the creation and maintenance of poverty.

But interconnectedness is real, as I discovered after eating some sushi. It was presented to me on a plastic tray which contained rice, fish, and a kind of radish called Wasabi. As I looked at the tray, I tried to imagine what would happen if time rolled backwards – a bit like playing a movie in reverse, starting at the present and rewinding the action towards the beginning.

In this movie the plastic tray was taken from me and eventually picked up by couriers and returned to a plastic factory. The factory returned plastic granules which were shipped back to the oil refinery. The refinery then returned it to the ocean-going tanker which travelled in reverse half way around the globe until it pumped  the oil back into the well. Then the oil well was undiscovered and the land restored to pristine condition.

It is simply astonishing how much ingenuity and energy went into putting this plastic tray on my table.

Then I looked at the fish reverse movie. The fish was uncut and put back together. Into a freezer it went, which was transported back to the harbour and loaded back into the fishing vessel. The fishing vessel then reversed to the lawless water of the Somalian fishing grounds, where in reverse it undid the destruction to the ocean floor, putting back every living thing it had previously raked off the ocean floor. This action then reversed and reduced the desperation of Somali fishermen, who had to turn to piracy because their fisheries were not plundered by foreign long-range fishing vessels. Then Somalia had a few less desperate people and returned to more bountiful, peaceful times.

Then I imagine that the rice returned to the cooking pot, before it is poured back into the bag. It was then transported back to the silo and from there back to the farm, where is sank back into the ground and where the irrigation water was returned to the thirsty dried-out Australian riverbeds.

This reversing, then, eventually restores the river flow to a point in time where it could flow again – supporting a multitude of life.

When we enjoy products, especially super-cheap or food "stuff", we never pay the full price, because many of the people who contributed to the making of our "stuff" are not paid their dues in either monetary or moral currency. Nor is the environmental destruction costed into our buying price. The consequences of stuff that is too cheap and its human, moral, environmental and peace-destroying side-effects are paid by someone else in a foreign place, or by someone less fortunate down the road who lives in a slum. Just because we pay for products does not mean that it is handed to us by an invisible hand, cleansed of all moral obligation.

Simple actions have big consequences, which we have to acknowledge and own. The triad of poverty, war and hunger mainly exists because it supports and pays for our own selfish "over the top" life style. But someone else is paying on our behalf. The Somali fisherman, turned lawless pirate, is paying with his life. Chinese plastic workers breathe polluted air and drink polluted water. Australian rice farmers go bankrupt because of climate change and market-driven, race to the bottom, corporate agricultural techniques.

The secret to understanding poverty lies with a term I coined: the *20 – 1000 law*. Say you participate in a reality business show, a la "Your fired!", where a sober-looking person asks you to embarrass yourself on TV, saying to you: "Would you drop your trousers – right here – right now, for $20? Naturally you would refuse the offer. Then the offer is raised: "Would you drop your trousers for $1,000?" and you would probably instantly reach for your belt buckle. But at that point, you are informed of two things:

a) that they have no inhibitions or morals and

b) that you are not thinking like a business person. Because $20 weekly for 50 weeks has a yearly value of $1,000. Applying business logic, both offers were identical. Applying emotions they look vastly different.

The point I am trying to make is that our small actions multiplied by millions or billions of people on this planet are identical in magnitude of damage and moral responsibility.

Just because you only eat a small piece of whale, does not mean that you have only a small piece of responsibility to carry. You carry the same load as the whaler.

The consequences of this effect are twofold. Firstly we need to look at the life-cycle of the "stuff" we consume. Secondly, we need to realise that our consumption produces unimaginably large profits which may end up in immoral and dangerous hands.

Careless consumption is like buying illegal drugs from a dealer. With drug profit, the dealer buys a trafficked sex worker, bribes politicians and police and terrorises the drug-producing nation with a drug war. The person who made this misery possible is the drug-user because his money gave the drug dealer the resources which are the foundation of his power. Who should than shoulder more blame – the drug consumer or the dealer?

It is a classic "What came first – the chicken or the egg?" question. Clearly, the dealer may have evil intents. But nothing can happen until he gets money or the opportunity to do it and both the money and opportunity are provided by the consumer of the drugs. Therefore, the consumer must carry the primary responsibility. The stuff you get to get high has consequences and you have sided with evil the moment you hand over your money. Body and soul, boots-n-all, you are hooked and totally responsible for the trail of misery it causes. In the case of our economic system, this means *us* and makes corporations the drug dealers.

If we really want to end poverty, starvation and wars, then we have to change some fundamental things about our individual and collective behavior. In a nutshell, and in no particular order of importance, it comes down to this:

*Vigilance:* we must begin to distrust power and to dissolve and dilute its influence through the PSP power sharing system. With PSPs in place, we can go about our daily tasks and, with minimal vigilance, govern our affairs, safe in the knowledge that the PSP watch-dog mechanism protects us from power-crazed tyrants.

*Personal responsibility/morals:* we must begin to understand the consequences of our consumption.

*Cui bono* who ultimately profits and derives the most power from our consumption and are we really happy with their ethics? We need to be sure, because we are handing them the tools and the power of life and death, with every purchase we make.

*Sustainable cities/villages*- Corporate overheads pay for our metropolises, which could not sustain themselves through their own efforts. Corporations only exist because they can siphon off a percentage of everyone else's labour.

However, our ancient, free city models are closest to how our sustainable future will look. Local security, civility, company, learning, arts, manufacture, food production, energy production, fair trade, waste and water management, defence, law and order are the cornerstones of a peaceful, sustainable future. Taxes should flow from the towns to the regional parliament, and then on to the national parliament. This reversed tax process would keep the "Dogs of War" firmly on the chain, because power is widely distributed and the resources needed for waging serious wars would be in the hands of the many– the people–and no longer solely controlled by vested parliamentary interest groups, lobby groups and political parties.

It is perfectly conceivable that we can quite quickly usher in the end of the old economic era – and the dawn of another. As the old system deteriorates, we have to distribute the right information to stop a decline into another Dark Age. I am talking about a process which could be forced through Satyagraha in a few years, or more sensibly and peacefully over a generation, and most probably will have run its course over a period of a few hundred years.

A Satyagraha is a mighty weapon and not a peaceful fluffy toy. This point must be fully appreciated, otherwise a Satyagraha could start a bloody civil war. I see Satyagraha like a Weapon of Mass Destruction - it is not harmless and it has mighty consequences for which we may not be ready. But where should we start? With our next soft-drink purchase? By becoming politically active? By reforming our councils? Through open government PSP style?

In fact, we can start anywhere and, if we feel the need to stop an aggressor, we can still start a serious Satyagraha about a specific issue – to topple the mighty – through boycotts. But we must realise that an all-out Satyagraha is a tool of last resort. The world is full of troubles and we don't need another match to ignite it further.

In India during the last few years leading into 2012, the Gandhian\ inspired activist, Anne Hazare who I mentioned in a previous chapter, has led an anti corruption campaign against the might of the Indian parliament. As a seventy-four year old pensioner, Hazare has about $1000 in his bank account and has for years given all surplus to village charities. He has led the Indian parliament on a merry dance through an on-and-off hunger strike to the death. His only other weapon is knowing how to use a Satyagraha and its powers are felt in over a billion households, day after day.

If a sprightly pensioner can make a billion people dance to his tune, using a Satyagraha, imagine what a handful of determined younger, more energetic, people can achieve, using the same peaceful methods.

But first we do need to form a clear picture of what we want to achieve. If we want to eliminate poverty and depravities cause by our thoughtless actions, then we also need to include the poor in our strategy. The world's poor also need to organise their affairs, so that they can help themselves. They need to become aware that our elite economic system is not their friend, but a tool of silent aggression against their interests.

Gandhi frequently warned about economic violence which deprives body and soul, for greedy gain. But the poor could act simply by not buying corporate products or be hard-nosed at getting a fair price for their labour and their raw materials and the food they grow. This does however mean protection of self interests and organised resistance, as concessions from the rich are only won after hard non-violent struggle. But, above all, they need to realise that the solutions to their problems are not all externally inflicted, but that they also lie   within themselves, and can   also largely   be solved by themselves and in their own communities.

This might sound harsh, given the scale of the problem, but we must remind ourselves that the poor are not stupid. They are simply trapped in poverty and ignorance with few opportunities to break free! But above all, we have to treat the rich and the poor with the same degree of dignity and extend the power and courtesy of natural justice equally to everyone.

We, as the world's elite, must also do our part because our own challenges are great, if not greater, than the ones faced by the poor. We must begin to build a new global dual economy – one for the rich and one for the poor, with a solid fence between the two! Our current economic system is built on greed and exploitation and is an ill match for poor countries, where the mass of the population has to deal with a daily struggle for survival. We have to make technology freely available to allow the Natural Economies of the world to develop a more people-friendly system based on small scale, local enterprises.

Our generosity should include a waver on pharmaceutical and general patents, as well as a one-way tariff-free, unlimited trade from poor economies to our "greed -based economies".

It is today fanciful to think that a Peace Corp could be used to troubleshoot humanitarian aid, education, water and food infrastructure as well as help in the establishment of peace zones in strife torn areas. But it is not impossible! We could start by diverting 10% of our huge war budgets to peace-building, and famine elimination efforts. We should not forget that Iraq was conquered in a few weeks, but that our armies have ZERO idea of how to secure peace and economic prosperity after the war. It is simply a skill that is totally lacking in our armies. Many soldiers I meet call themselves peacekeepers. Sure, peace can be kept pointing the barrel of a gun at trouble spots. But the same skill could be used to secure peace on two fronts: economically, to fill stomachs, and militaristically, to shield against aggressors. Rome prospered for millennia because it was an agrarian, military and inclusive society.

Food, trade, arts and security build the Roman Empire, whereas, inherited privilege, limited upward mobility, poverty, racism and idleness led to its destruction.

If we truly want peace, then we must first ensure that our war-based elite economies keep on producing and consuming armaments. We need to understand that these powerful players are not going to simply go away. They too have families to feed and stock market shareholders to appease. We should begin by opening a new income stream for the armaments industry like training and supplying Peace Corps. This might in time open not just a new income stream to make more profits, but become an alternative income stream, which replaces, for example, the money made from land-mines.

A quick calculation reveals that almost the entire armaments industry could be kept busy for many decades, if not for centuries – simply by supplying Peace Corps with the tools and skills to build safe, self-sustaining communities in troubled places around the globe, totally replacing and overtaking profits derived from armaments manufacturing.

Peace is a tough issue, but we should remember that we can't build peace by giving our neighbours a bloody nose. We currently don't have enough faith in ourselves to begin changing our methods from aggression to peace building. Instead we are used to going in, Rambo-style, with guns blazing. We don't have the courage to go in with an extended helping hand, offering peace and security for those who crave it and a stern deterrent to those who are hell-bent on destruction.

Then larger again looms the issue of taking responsibility for our personal consumption and for our greed, which fuels our growth-based elite economies. We should scale back our consumption to a small-town, self-reliant, model, which can self-sustain small populations and deal with its pollution in its own environment.

The concept of an Economic Satyagraha, in our advanced economies simply means "green living" and power sharing, whereas in the "natural economies" it stands for power, pride and self-reliance.

You might have already noticed the 800 pound gorilla that I have avoided mentioning; namely, how to deal with power abuse and corruption. This point is, however, covered in the PSP (people sharing incorruptible power) book.

As time passes, and if good people choose to act morally, the extremes between the rich and poor will one day be history. But this is the story of another time and another age. In the meantime, we have to rediscover our morality and begin to confront and tame the driving forces of poverty, war and hunger. Us!

We only enjoy a brief "moment of consciousness" on our beautiful planet, before we turn to dust. Let's make it a memorable and worthwhile "walk of consciousness"!

We are at a turning point in history. A time like BC and AD. Our times may one day be called BP and AP. *Before Poverty* and *After Poverty*. It's quaint to remember that BC and AD were named after a carpenter. The ultimate power of one...well, actually three. The Nurturer, the Son, and a fabulous high moral idea. But I digress...

# Do we have any values at all?

There is a notable change in how we view the world now to the way we saw it as little as forty years ago. In the sixties, we believed in an upbeat power that is summarised in the following speech. It contrasts sharply with our personal and public/political sentiments and actions after 2000.

*'Man holds in his mortal hands the power to abolish all forms of human poverty and all forms of human life. And yet the same revolutionary beliefs for which our forebears fought are still at issue around the globe – the belief that the rights of man come not from the generosity of the state, but from the hand of God.'*

These sentiments distinguish the statement as upbeat sixties because it acknowledges that natural justice is a birth right instead of something that comes with privilege and wealth.

*'Let the word go forth from this time and place, to friend and foe alike, that the torch has been passed to a new generation of Americans – born in this century, tempered by war, disciplined by a hard and bitter peace, proud of our ancient heritage – and unwilling to witness or permit the slow undoing of those human rights to which this Nation has always been committed, and to which we are committed today at home and around the*

*world.'*

Ironically we have done the opposite and have cheapened humanity in the name of economic growth and greed. The growth the USA experienced in the post was year was however repeated time and again around the globe through a Harvard business hegemony of economic exploitation of less developed nations.

*'Let every nation know, whether it wishes us well or ill, that we shall pay any price, bear any burden, meet any hardship, support any friend, oppose any foe, in order to assure the survival and the success of liberty.*

*This much we pledge - and more.'*

*To those new States whom we welcome to the ranks of the free, we pledge our word that one form of colonial control shall not have passed away merely to be replaced by a far more iron tyranny.'*

I wonder if the economic hegemony imposed by the USA in the post-war years around the world, could be the iron tyranny that economic hot heads like Bin Laden took objection to when declaring war against the west and its business class. Whilst he was a multimillionaire heir and his family had business ties with Saudi's ruling class, he was also critical of the treatment and disinterest Saudi rulers dished out the the poor. It is well documented that Bin Laden's religiously inspired benevolence of the poor was on a hard collision course with Saudi's elite. It is a little know fact that Bin Laden trained in part as an economist and only later found his remedy to the misery he saw being inflicted on the Muslim world, in reestablishing the old geographic range and influence of the Ottoman's Kaffir Muslim empire and Sharia Law. He has also some teachers who were members of the Muslim brotherhood, who were said to have led to his radicalisation.

In any case, economics have replaced older methods of oppression and exploitation. It's just a lot harder to spot when the oppressor waves a corporate check book instead of a gun in your face. Gandhi made it very clear that aggression and violence can hide behind many masks and economics is one of the smartest looking masks and one of the hardest to spot weapons of violence.

*'We shall not always expect to find them supporting our view. But we shall always hope to find them strongly supporting their own freedom - and to remember that, in the past, those who foolishly sought power by riding the back of the tiger ended up inside.*

*To those peoples in the huts and villages across the globe struggling to break the bonds of mass misery, we pledge our best efforts to help them help themselves, for whatever period is required - not because the Communists may be doing it, not because we seek their votes, but because it is right. If a free society cannot help the many who are poor, it cannot save the few who are rich.'*

Ironically, in India, which perfectly fits the bill of the speech, the rich are getting richer and the poor, especially farmers, are suiciding at a rate of over one thousand per year because their livelihoods has been destroyed by our Free Trade economic system. So how exactly are we helping them in 2012? It's more the case of the poor helping us unwittingly by contributing profits to our economic system which maintains our lifestyle!

*'So let us begin anew – remembering on both sides that civility is not a sign of weakness, and sincerity is always subject to proof. Let us never negotiate out of fear. But let us never fear to negotiate.*

How poorly our leaders and our own morals today contrast with the aspirations of a nation in 1961. But to what extend did Kennedy really voice the thoughts and aspirations of corporate America or even the bulk of ordinary Americans? He had a good speech writer. I often feel it is the speechwriters who should be getting the praise for these great speeches. But in the end it was Kennedy who mastered the reading and delivery that transcended a simple political show into the stuff of legends.

Theodore Chaikin Sorensen, was credited with having mingled his prose with the thoughts and words of his close friend John F. Kennedy to create some of the most memorable presidential speeches of the 20th century. While editing this section, I learned by coincidence that he died today, 7-03-2012, nine days after suffering a stroke.

Mr. Sorensen's wife, Gillian, said he died at noon in a hospital in New York City of complications from the stroke. It is ironic to think that his close friend Kennedy died in part from the complications and fervour of their inspiring speeches. A tragic case of shooting the messenger.

This speech shows how low we have sunk in our own esteem of human kindness. Kennedy's assassination was not just the death of a man – it was the death of a dream and even more sadly the foundation of a higher heartless iron tyranny. Economics!

*'Now the trumpet summons us again - not as a call to bear arms, though arms we need; not as a call to battle, though embattled we are - but a call to bear the burden of a long twilight struggle, year in and year out, "rejoicing in hope, patient in tribulation" - a struggle against the common enemies of man: tyranny, poverty, disease, and war itself.'*

*'My fellow citizens of the world: ask not what America will do for you, but what together we can do for the freedom of man.'*

Inaugural Address by John F. Kennedy - January 20th 1961 I read Kennedy's reference to a *"more iron tyranny"* as referring to our industrialized economies and unconscionable stock market exploits and deem his prophetic fears to have come true for the poor of the world.

What are we as individuals willing to do and willing to forego in the name of justice and for the love of humanity? In truth, all we have to do to change world history is to spend our money wisely, to embrace PSPs and perhaps start believing that we can take care of our own destiny, without cowering in the shadows of corporations.

Kennedy dreamt of a new world order and painted a picture of a future that the post-war generations could create.

Today's leaders paint a picture not with the colours of human warmth and ingenuity but with an ink made from a dark self-serving hunger for power. They depict a future and paint it with imaginary blood. Australians largely have bought into their leaders' vision and policies of fear without any questioning. Today's Australians mindlessly accept this vision and kow-tow to baseless fears, having been made pliable by imaginary visions of violence and potential fears that are more real to us than reality itself. We fear boat people, immigrants, crime, terrorism, war, and medical and environmental catastrophes. In reality, we should fear alcohol and tobacco more than all the above together, because these two kill more of us in a single year than all our imaginary fears and real foes do in a decade.

In the end, it comes down to us doing and believing what we are told by our leaders and by the corporate mass media. The proud, fearless Australian iconoclasts of yore have spawned a new generation of spineless jelly, molded by fear, intellectual laziness and political indifference. We are now a people who are too smug to make a fuss by speaking out and too lazy to act on our convictions.

# Religion and natural justice

---

Philosophy and religion have since time immemorial tried to define that unique quality which makes us human. At a time when religion is in decline in the modern, technologically-savvy world, we should not think that religion is just *'the opium of the masses'*. Instead of ignoring religion, we should use it to re-ignite a sense of awe that surrounds every living thing.

The search for meaning in our lives has undergone a dramatic change. We saw ourselves in early earth-mother religions as a product of nature. We marveled at the transformation from dirt into a conscious human being, which, at the end of its life, decomposed back into earth. Our actions and thoughts were intertwined with the bounty and random cruelty of nature. We acted like naughty children and offered appeasements to our parents – the spirit water god in the sky and the mother god of the earth. Separately, they were just water and lifeless dirt. But once they consummated their love with thunder and lightning, they spawned us. We then repeated this cycle of life and, when we climaxed during intercourse, we saw a repeat of the rumble and lightning of our gods' lovemaking and realised that we too had the divine spark of life within our own earthly vessels.

Millennia have passed and our major religions define now a single, supernatural omnipotent being as God. The union of the Ying and the Yang has lost its importance. So what has changed? The simple answer is that a concentration of power has taken place that has usurped the old gods. Now we worship corporations and their trinkets! A belief system which sees a divine spark in every human and every human as a child of God also makes every human a divinity and thus makes every human equal. The divinity in every human is a dangerous concept because it breaks up power and throws doubt on any human's claim to superiority. The key to understanding a decline of religion and morals in advanced economies lies in our concept of personal freedom. Our own level of experiencing freedom and satisfaction are bound up with power and money – and both power and money are symbols of superiority.

Therefore, if we judge our success on power and money, then morals, religion and human equality are opposing concepts which we, as well-heeled First World people, have to reject in order to maintain a belief in ourselves and our actions. We have therefore constructed a society on an artifice which has lost contact with the divine spark in humanity and we therefore have become comfortable enough to deny some humans their just claim to equality.

It is hard for us as individuals to judge the enormity of the power we grant to unscrupulous political and economic leaders. We grant them this power not only by casting a democratic vote, but more importantly by following a path of consumerism which is laid out for us from cradle to grave. We empower our leader with every unthinking purchase and disempower them when we make a conscious purchase from a better alternative. The ultimate power that is generated on earth comes from our consumption and our unwillingness to take moral responsibility for the consequences.

But the meaning of life should concerns us, because it is defines not only ourselves but also points to a larger truth.

I am especially moved by the mix of religion and proof-based beliefs of American Indians. They too regarded every human as a god but, in addition, also placed every human being in the centre of the entire universe. Their proof was simply this: open your eyes and look all around you – up into the sky and down to the ground. You are the centre of the universe as you comprehend it. Then close your eyes and imagine you die and the universe has died with you. You are also a god, because you were, as religion explains, created in the image of God because a child is a copy of its parents.

This simple, logical and simultaneously profound image of humans as gods puts a totally different meaning on how we relate to people. When we kill, we destroy a god. When we are impolite, maim, starve or mistreat a person, we not only interfere with that person's divinity we also inhibit this divinity from fully reaching its potential. We cannot imagine someone disfiguring, burning, defecating on or even verbally blaspheming, burning a Crucifix, Bible or Koran. Any of these acts are unthinkable and would draw instant outrage, contempt and hate for the perpetrator. However, we are quite willing to tolerate the same foul actions in the name of religious and economic wars. We willingly exploit and demean other human beings but we cowardly shield our emotions from reality. How different would we view the loss of life, if we looked at every human being as a god walking with a unique and irreplaceable identity among many gods?

We are part of a planet that is a blue living jewel in a dead universe. Even for agnostics, who happily live without religion, there is a divine sanctity in living things' in general, and especially in human consciousness. Who has not been astonished, when holding a few handfuls of dirt, that it can transform itself to food which gives rise to us as sentient beings? Who is not awed when holding this dirt and realizing that it holds the building blocks from which we are made?

However, to elite economists who participate in the violation of human rights, the meaning of life is an economic unit of consumption, which can be measured, studied and analyzed. It can be exploited for the common good of the world's nations or be narcissistically exploited for the pleasures of the world's elite. Because you are reading this text, and because you probably sleep in a bed, have a sound roof over your head and eat several times a day, this probably includes you, irrespective of your gender, colour or religious bent. Morals are simple truths. You cannot eat small piece of chicken without killing the entire chicken. So your guilt weights as heavily as the butcher's, as there is no logical separation between killing and eating chicken.

If there is to be any deeper meaning to our life, it is found in the reflection we create in the mirror of other people. We need the common people – the unloved, unknown and unimportant people – to give meaning to our life. They lift you to your greatest heights and drop you into your deepest despairs. It is the mirror of the common people that makes us feel important and it is they who destroy us when they choose to shun or ignore us.

Can you imagine a politician standing in an empty hall, or a dictator yelling, "Wollt Ihr den totalen Krieg ?" into an empty Nuremberg stadium? A rock diva, dressed to the nines, emerging from a stretch limousine to walk a red carpet and not one, not even a single paparazzi, shows up? People are mirrors which return to us the image our actions create in them.

If we measured the value of our existence in the good we do for other people, then our material wealth makes it possible to create a positive image of ourselves in the joy we bring to others. But who are the others, the throngs of the unloved and unwashed, who hold the key to our self worth? What makes us personally so different to the great masses of humanity? Is it our superior intellect or our manipulative ways that makes us different to poor people?

However, we forget that there is a place where everyone is equal. When you draw your last breath and drift into the white light, you will be nothing, and when the last person who knew you during your life is also dead, you will be unknown, unloved, unimportant and nothing more than egalitarian dust!

With this sobering view of life, elitist thinking, exploitative economics, hording of unrealistic wealth and conspicuous consumption of wealth is not just obscene, it is downright sad! It is attention-seeking of the worst kind. But, as a society, we celebrate the *Nirvana of glamorous conspicuous consumption* in our magazines, books, movies and in the mass media. We accept a perversion of basic human needs and accept the egotistic celebrity status which is implied in our conspicuous consumerism. Native people all around the world figured out religion and inter-human relationships millennia ago, whereas most of us today are just hollow moral vessels adrift in a river of moral obscenities and selfish, self-justified desires.

Another interesting way to look at humanity is to describe and see ourselves as twilight beings. In this world view, we live neither in bright daylight nor in the total darkness of night. We can only exist in the now, which is the precarious position of twilight. We live on the border between the past and the future. We can neither return to the past, nor stop ourselves from hurtling into the future. The future comes with or without us, while the past cannot have existed without us. We are time lords. Everyone a god. Everyone stands on the mountaintop which is the hub of the universe and the world which revolves around us.

Yet, strangely, we don't ever see ourselves as gods of time. We see ourselves more like driftwood in the mighty river of time. We accept that we have to go with the flow of the river. Thus, we deny ourselves an important divine potential – namely our ability to shape the future. We can dream of time travel yet strangely we are time travelers in denial.

Just imagine we could return to a point in time when an evil person was about to be conceived. If we could ring the door bell and interrupt the couple who were about to create this future evil doer, we could prevent world wars, world hunger and accomplish many other good things. We would truly be gods. However, this is the paradox of our existence! We are actually time travelers. We may not appreciate our divine gift, but we do travel always into the future and we actually can predict and shape the future. We can prevent many ugly things from actually occurring in the future.

Sadly, we have forgotten the power of the god that is inside every one of us. We have become unthinking, morally dead driftwood that goes with the flow! What a magnificent being any one of us could be, if we became aware of our powers as time lords.

I return to the future when I restate my original opening statement: *The meaning of life is an economic unit of consumption, which can be measured, studied, analysed and exploited for the common good of the world's nations, or it can be narcissistically exploited for the pleasures of the world's elite.*

Are we just driftwood that goes with the flow of the Harvard business school of economic rationalism? Are we not more than the sum of our economic parts? Is our existence not miraculous and our consciousness a mystery?

Can we afford to forget that the divine gift of our consciousness exists only for a very short period of time before we return to actual dust?

Our chance to shape the future is limited to a short period in time. Consider the dirt we are made of and consider the chances of these materials ever reuniting again in exactly the same way to form another you? We will never be conscious again but will blend back into the consciousness of *Gaia*. Our time to exist and be gods is now! We alone on our planet hold the key to the meaning of life and we should use it to unlock the treasures of life. We should accept that we only exist to shape the future.

It appears as if the forces which have created our planet and which gave it the spark of life, have given us the poison chalice of consciousness. The meaning of life concerns us, because it is us. We are the centre of the universe and every one of us is a God, because we were created in the image of God. We are the only part of nature which has the divine power to shape the future of our planet. We are all time travelers whizzing through space on a planet which is a rare blue jewel in an otherwise lifeless universe. Whatever we decide – whether it a good deed or passive inaction to an injustice – we personally will enjoy or suffer the consequences, because we alone have the power to shape the future and Economic Satyagraha is the tool to get the job done.

If 'Animal farm' has tough us anything then it is this:

All human ambitions turn to dust – only some are dustier than others!

# *Dreams of world domination are not new*

Antonio de Pereda , (Valladolid 1611-1678 Madrid),Allegory of Vanity

Are you dreaming of world domination, empire building, wealth, status, power and glory? If you answer yes, then Pereda's allegory was painted for you!

Pereda tells us that the hourglass and the skulls should remind us of the futility of our ambitions because in the end all of our ambitions turn to dust. Just look into the angel's face – note the raised eyebrows, the bemused questioning facial expression that has *"heard it all before."*

She appears to be asking: *"...and what have you been up to with your time on earth? What have you done with the gift of consciousness?"* She knows already that all of God's children's endeavours turn to dust.

Pereda, to be sure that the viewer gets the point of the allegory, painted the answer to the angel's question between the skull and the hourglass. It looks like it has been irreverently scratched into the table with the skull's teeth:

" *Nil omne* " All is vanity !

...because the only thing that will remain of you is the most egalitarian of things – dust!

Allegories of vanity, depicting status, wealth and power, contrasted with death and time slipping away, were favorite themes even way back in Roman times. They were frequently used as wall paintings in Roman banquet halls. It was a reminder to have fun and a reminder to be wary of vain ambitions.

Throughout history, allegories of vanity served as warnings for the rich and the powerful to ponder on death and to remind us all of the miracle of life. How can we, bags of flesh and bones, actually believe we have any real power? All that we can hope for is the experience of life with its richness, joys and sorrows. If along the way we help to carry someone else's burden, then we have stepped beyond the beast and inched closer to a true love of humanity.

So, what went wrong with us? Have we ever looked at an allegory and pondered the meaning of our existence? Have we forgotten that the preservation of life is the purpose of living?

Blinded by the pursuit of power we uphold an economic system which causes harm to millions of people. But life is not a football game that can be won! Our wealth and power won't prolong our lives for long and even if one day science could clone our consciousness into a new body and let us live forever, would we have truly lived without the certainty of death?

Is dying and the turning to dust where we should look for the afterlife? Should we begin to view our planet as paradise and the dust below our feet as the repository of our consciousness that one day will again turn into the building blocks that spark new life in all its infinite variety and splendor?

*"He who is not angry when there is just cause for anger is immoral. Why? Because anger looks to the good of justice. And if you can live amid injustice without anger, you are immoral as well as unjust."*

-Aquinas, 1225-1274, Father of natural, western theology.

*"When the same man, or set of men, holds the sword and the purse, there is an end of liberty."*

-George Mason 1725-1792, Father of the USA's Bill of Rights.

# *Natural Justice as a moral foundation for a just rage*

---

Lysander Spooner, advocate of natural justice and America's first monopoly breaker.

A stamp from his failed attempt to break the postal monopoly.

At last we have come to the main point of this book.

On what grounds can we justify messing with our social system? What gives us the right to rebel against our rulers? How can we ensure that what we feel in our hearts is a just rage and not a foolish idealistic, easily dismissed sentiment?

Desmond Tutu

Those of us who have achieved public recognition can easily give and express our opinions. Our fame or infamy gives our opinions weight and what we say is taken seriously. But what of those among us who are just another face in a pool of billions. What can we do to give our opinions weight? What do we have to do to be taken seriously?

There was an incident in President Obama's White House campaign. A tradesman was called upon to give evidence in public to score a political point. This guy was not referred to as Mr Smith of XYZ town, who has made a serious contribution to the debate. Rather, he was ridiculed as a 'Bob the Plumber' type of pleb. This ordinary guy's contribution was easily marginalised and made fun off. The point is this. If an ordinary person wants to be taken seriously, then they have to throw verbal firecracker that hit the target and make our opponents' arguments look immature and stupid.

I had a strange encounter with some politicians, as a participant of a TV show named Q&A. This show is a type of political blood sport. Public personalities, opinion makers and politicians are invited to answer blunt questions from the audience. I was lucky and my question about political donations, which are a public form of bribery in Australia, was put to the then shadow attorney-general of Australia, George Brandis. Also present was the then Queensland state premier Anna Bligh, who was battling bribery allegations that same week.

Paraphrased, here is what I asked: *"At what point does lobbying end and corruption start? When undisclosed party donation below $11,000 are handed over, or when the doors to "off the record" meetings are shut?"*

Both politicians on the panel were from opposing political parties – but both defended this institutionalised system of bribery which is conducted under the guise of political party fundraising. The shadow attorney especially made the argument, which I paraphrase again, that *it is necessary that political parties can accept unlimited donation and that it is a bookkeeping imposition to have to declare donation below $11,000.* I replied, in essence, that a small business person would have to go jail if they did not disclose income, and that $11,000 is not a small amount for the average Australian, and that he was championing two laws for the Australian people – one for the rich and another for the poor. He went mad and verbally dug himself deeper and deeper into an indefensible position. --The Queensland premier, to her credit, later changed a law, started an inquiry that looked at donations and political outcomes and promised to put the issue on the national political agenda when she ascends to the federal presidency of her party.

Naturally I was not alone in kicking this goal. There were many like-minded people working to place the ball within reach of the goal post. Also, the host Tony Jones was an expert journalistic inquisitor. He cleverly maximised the fallout.

But why did so many unconnected people agree with these anti-corruption questions and why were so many people simultaneously outraged over our politicians' behavior? This is a question worth asking. What was the origin of our collective outrage? What channeled the emotions related to this issue to make me ask this question? Where did I pick up on these vibes? The answer is childishly simple. Grandmother might have called it: "What's good for the goose is good for the gander!" I had simply based my question and arguments on the principles of natural justice. Natural justice is, to every human, as simple as breathing and the knowledge that we all deserve to breathe clean air. So when someone suggests that poor people should only breathe dirty air, then this causes us instinctively to take offence.

Exposing simple truths that are based on natural justice is the foundation that wins any serious argument.

Just as a by-note: This fifteen-second exchange on national TV had two other public speakers pick up the same argument within days. One was a union leader who argued for the same wages for the same work. The other was made by a bikie gang leader who argued that a proposed special anti-bikie gang law that treats gang members differently to other citizens is a breach of natural justice. But this was a fallacious argument because the attention they had drawn to themselves that caused the change in law, was caused by a vicious public gang fight at Sydney airport. Natural justice did not bite as an argument, because it was a law and order issue and not a simple denial of natural justice.

The art of economic politics and leadership is to form arguments that confuse or mislead us into accepting falsehoods as truths, and limited, often stupid choices, as the only viable alternatives. I am surprised that Hitler did not say: *"Do you want to just invade Poland or do you want all-out war?"* The current issue of carbon trading is another example of such a conjuring trick. We are led to believe that we must force a new tax on people so that our big polluters can trade this new source of income on a carbon stock market and that the urgent adoption of this plan is vital if we want to save our planet! These kinds of intrinsically dumb statements are the hallmarks of accomplished politicians and often the handiwork of focus groups and spin doctors.

To illustrate the danger of spin let me state unambiguously that there is no material or logical distinction between commerce, war and human rights (oops, I myself just slipped into danger spin – darn!)

To clarify this point, let me define the link between Natural Justice and Economic Satyagraha, by reinterpreting the meaning and nature of the inalienable concepts of natural justice embedded therein. But let me first clear up why smarter, stronger humans should not, in Darwinian terms, dominate and destroy the "less well adapted"? Gandhi offers us the answer on a plate. In his mind, humanity evolved into the dominant species on earth because we were are peace-loving and sociable. And the peaceful have survived and prospered in far greater numbers than the aggressive. Society anywhere is proof that we mostly get along fine, even when there are millions of us living in a metropolis. Had evolution favored the strong and aggressive, we would never have gone past the state of the savanna warlord. So you could argue that if nature favors the meek and mild, it also infers that it prefers them as they are closer to nature's ideal image of itself!

Natural justice for me means that every human is an integral part of nature, that our planet is a gift to all people and when we deny even one human being a fair existence, we destroy nature, its diversity and beauty itself. Therefore, a denial of any person's natural justice must be strongly resisted because it is immoral as well as unjust.

Every human has the birthright to partake in fair and equal measure of our planet's life-sustaining resources, which nature's bounty has provided free for all of its creations. As nature's secrets are unraveled through science and inventions, every human has an equal right to its benefits because science too is a gift of nature. Every human has, therefore, the right to live in equal peace, free from oppression and curable diseases. Furthermore, everyone has the right to share in technologies which enrich our lives and liberate us from being mere beasts of burden.

Nature has provided us with wealth-creation mechanisms which are related to human consumption. It is immoral to monopolize the harvesting and distribution of this wealth because it deprives humanity of resources which stop it from reaching its innate potential and reduces and debases humans to be mere wage slaves and values them only as "units of economic consumption".

Natural justice also demands that every human must extent the same rights to every other human being to enable everybody to reach and enjoy his or her full potential. But above all, we must be good caretakers of the multitudes of live-forms which inhabit our planet because all life is related and the extinctions of species, and careless use of nature's capital resources, may eventually doom humanity itself.

If we are to launch a serious attempt to end poverty then we need a sound moral foundation to carry our convictions. We need a moral as well as a logical foundation which lets us win argument at work, for fun or in Parliament. The history of natural justice is as old as humanity. It was with us at the dawn of our consciousness and it is still instilled in us with our mother's milk. But we have lost focus and can no longer answer the simple question: "What is a just rage and where does our authority to act on it come from?"

Let's wind the clock back and search for the origin of natural justice. Where do the ancient roots of our just rage come from?

To answer these questions, let me introduce Lysander Spooner and Desmond Tutu as two of the finest champions of natural justice. Looking at them in the above pictures, one would not know that they are two superstars of natural justice. It is hard to understand why they are so important. Neither became famous through infamy, but both inspired millions to act within the spirit of natural justice.

To paraphrase Lysander Spooner: Children, anywhere, eventually ask the same questions of their parents: Why can't we live in peace? What is war? Why are there so many poor people and why do so many people die of hunger?

The answers we get are slightly different for every child, depending on where they live and under which circumstances they live. But all children eventually have to learn and accept a bitter truth: namely, that we are little people who have no power, who must be obedient and who acknowledge that we can't change the world.

For many of us, this turning point heralds the end of our childhood and ends our childish innocence and a growing awareness and acceptance of injustice! We learn to rationalise injustices and accept our place in society! But, as we enter adulthood, we leave something very important behind. Namely, our intuitive understanding and love of natural justice!

When we were children in the playground, we would rally to the defense of friends who were unjustly treated. We would call for justice without being aware of the social status of the wrongdoer, or the consequences of our demands. We would accept nothing less than an apology and the payment of a fair compensation in order to make peace.

Every human being has a birthright to justice, peace and life-sustaining resources, which are in plentiful supply on our planet and are a free gift of nature to feed and sustain all of humanity. These are the simple, principle foundation stones of natural justice. But, as we enter adult life, we leave behind our childish ideas of natural justice and start believing in, and finding our place in, an economic system which kills 11 million people through starvation every year! (Estimates vary between 7 and 32 million. Only 8% of these deaths are attributed to drought (UNICEF). The majority die of systematically enforced starvation and preventable diseases! In the end it comes down to a systematic denial of work and the economic, life-sustaining benefits it brings to the poor.

Half of the world's population lives on less than $2 per day. (This calculation is based on the assumption that a $2 can of soft-drink costs $2 anywhere in the world. Not, as is often thought, that $2 in China buys the family meal and only buys a can of soft drink in the USA.)

But more serious than these cruelties against our fellow human beings is our firm believe that our economic system, and we ourselves, are not to blame. But rather, many are inclined to believe that it is the laziness of the poor and corruption which have entirely caused their unfortunate, but self-inflicted, poverty. It is this conservative economic ideology that clouds our understanding of poverty's real causes and robs us of an understanding of how we are personally involved in its workings. Most of us are especially ignorant of the fact that our own personal consumption, wasteful consumerism and wealth aspirations, have caused a credit bubble (sub-prime mortgage) which is ultimately paid for us by the things that we deny to the world's poor.

Let me go back in time and shine a light on Desmond Tutu. Archbishop Desmond Tutu's South African Truth and Reconciliation Commission is a good example of how natural justice can defuse dangerous situations. The Commission heard evidence from victims and from perpetrators of apartheid violence. Perpetrators were given amnesty from prosecution. The simple fact of hearing admissions of crimes, even though no punishment could be dealt out, often cleared the air and avoided future conflicts. It also gave solace to the victims and their families. The Commission was at the time criticised for being a toothless tiger which could only dish out tongue-lashings. One should, however, remember what Tutu himself said about this issue:

> *"It appears a soft option to simply give a criminal immunity from prosecution. This is however not the case. To step into a witness box and to confront their victims and their families in public view and confessing to atrocities is far harder than servicing a prison sentence."*

Many criminal, however, did not say sorry (which was optional) and claimed that they only followed state-sanctioned orders. Many, nevertheless, felt a release and asked their victims for forgiveness.

The following excerpt from the Zionist Organization of America shows how justice is never negotiable and above politics. A thing is either just or unjust and no amount of wishful thinking or political manoeuvrings can change that.

April 29, 2002 the New York – The Zionist Organization of America (ZOA) is urging Jewish allies of South African Archbishop Desmond Tutu to publicly protest Tutu's latest anti-Jewish and anti-Israel slurs. The Israeli daily Haaretz (April 29, 2002), reported Tutu's remarks at a recent conference in Boston and quoted him drawing on natural justice. Tutu said:

*"Israel is like Hitler and apartheid: I've been deeply distressed in my visit to the Holy Land; it reminded me so much of what happened to us black people in South*

*Africa. I have seen the humiliation of the Palestinians at checkpoints and roadblocks, suffering like us when young white police officers prevented us from moving about. I say why are our memories so short? Have our Jewish sisters and brothers forgotten their humiliation? Have they forgotten the collective punishment, the home demolitions, in their own history so soon? The apartheid government was very powerful, but today it no longer exists. Hitler, Mussolini, Stalin, Pinochet, Milosevic, and Idi Amin were all powerful, but in the end they bit the dust. Injustice and oppression will never prevail.*

*\* The Jewish lobby is very powerful: People are scared in this country [the U.S.], to say wrong is wrong because the Jewish lobby is powerful—very powerful.*

*Critics of Israel are being smeared: You know as well as I do that, somehow, the Israeli government is placed on a pedestal [in the U.S.] and to criticize it is to be immediately dubbed anti-Semitic, as if Palestinians were not Semitic."*

In reply, Morton A. Klein, National President of the Zionist Organization of America (ZOA), said: *"As a child of Holocaust survivors, I am deeply offended by Archbishop Tutu's vicious libel that Israel is comparable to Hitler. He should be speaking out against Yasir*(sic) *Arafat, who has murdered more Jews than anyone since Hitler; who has fostered a culture of anti-Jewish hatred in his schools, speeches, summer camps, religious sermons, and media."* Tutu lost a lot of friends by basing his arguments on the principle of natural justice. The Zionists argued that their position is just, since they suffered at an earlier time. But one cannot undo an injustice by linking it to an unrelated event – namely, the establishments of the state of Israel on land that belonged to the Palestinians. Cross-linking injustices simply creates another injustice. Whilst Israel feels the unjust killing of its citizens, the Palestinians and their Arab allies still smart from the injustice of colonialism, the recent occupation of Palestinian territory and their treatment under the rules of the occupation. While both parties are justly aggrieved, neither addresses the real issue. Namely the restoration of natural justice!

What is clearly lacking here on both sides is an appreciation of the principles of natural justice. Without addressing the issue of justice – on both sides – there can only be an escalation of the sense of injustice, which leads to further wars.

In the 2006 war between Lebanon and Israel, I overheard a young Australian of Lebanese descent say *"..but the Israeli kidnapped some Hesb'Allah men first and we only kidnapped their soldiers to have our men released."*

Clearly both sides of the conflict draw on heartfelt sentiments, which are deeply rooted in an apparent injustice. Does justice always have to be won by winning a war? Is it not logical to establish a mechanism which can deal with the issue of injustice before it turns to war? Terrorism, when viewed in this context, is a frustration caused by a denial of natural justice. It is, therefore, paradoxically truthful when we hear Arab commentators say that: *"Terrorism is not a sign of strength, but a sign of weakness! and frustration.* "It is obvious that, when conflicts are viewed as a matter of justice, actions aimed to restore natural justice can help to diffuse dangerous situations. But, sadly, we all too often prefer other alternatives like genocide or military intervention. It is part of our human condition that we will cry out for justice to our dying breath, beyond death and through the millennia.

**Justice is as important to us as the air we breathe!**

---

*"If there be such a principle as justice, or natural law, it ...tells us what rights were given to every human being at his birth ...what rights are, therefore, inherent in him as a human being, what rights will remain with him during life; and, however capable of being trampled upon, are incapable of being blotted out, extinguished, annihilated, or separated or eliminated from his nature as a human being, or deprived of their inherent authority or obligation.*

*If however, If there be no such science as justice, there can be no just ... government; and all the rapacity and violence, by which, in all ages and nations, a few confederated villains have obtained the mastery over the rest of mankind ... reduced them to poverty and slavery, and established what they called governments to keep them in subjection."* Lysander Spooner. 1808-1887.

To conclude, I draw on medieval history. In my example, I use a small German town which today barely numbers two thousand people but still bears witness to the power of natural justice.

Kindelbrueck is an attractive ancient and, to this day, walled city. It is a good example of a self-sufficient small agrarian/trading town, which did not have the need to grow larger because the locals were living in a comfortable, economic equilibrium.

In the year 1291 Kindelbrueck became a free city by

accident. The local burgers went to Landgraf Albrecht to seek justice. They won their plea/case and were awarded free town rights for their peasant settlement Kindelbrueck. In truth, it took many, many decades for the locals to comprehend the magnitude and value of this compensatory gift. But when they finally woke up to their economic power of self-government, the euphoria and harmony lasted nearly seven hundred years.

What happened opens an interesting insight into the workings of natural justice. Albrecht's over-zealous tax collectors had unjustly extorted excessive taxes from the peasant settlement. The heavy burden of this tax caused the locals many hardships. The incredible thing about this incident is that the peasants were in bondage. They were owned body and soul by Albrecht. This alone posed an interesting question. If these people were serfs and totally owned, body and soul, by their lord, what gave them the right to seek compensation from their owner?

The answer lies in part in the natural law of the land called locally the "Recht des guten Grundes" or as we know it in the English-speaking world, natural law, natural justice or the irrefutable law of reason and the ancient law of common sense.Kings were subject to the same law as common people. Kings were regarded as the guardian of the people's law. When we think of Lords or Kings, we think of them today as omnipotent law-makers. But for a long time they were law keepers and the upholders of the ancient law of irrefutable common sense. Natural justice. Kings who made new laws or broke with natural law were simply called tyrants and were able to be deposed by a new just king and law keeper.

It is interesting to note that even as recently as immediately before the French Revolution, commoners would burst uninvited into the king's sleeping chamber at the palace of Versailles to demand justice. But when the people cried in hunger for food and were given the royal answer to eat cake, tyrants' heads soon rolled.

The people of Kindelbrueck were the king's moral equals because they all accepted that they shared an equal birthright to natural justice. However, they realised they needed protection and that this obliged them to pay their king's taxes which would be used wisely to defend their interests and to maintain justice. They bowed their heads and submitted to a form of economic exploitation and subjugation. But this subjugation had moral limits and, when these limits were transgressed, even powerless serfs could demand restorative justice from their kings. As time passed, religion combined with power and turned the kings into omnipotent representatives of God. Kings gradually changed the ancient relationship by exchanging the morals of natural justice with the morals of religion and a rule by force. Gradually, the benign just kings and free city merchants changed into tyrants who drew their strength from the people's economic output.

This marks the point in humanity's evolution where we discarded natural justice and embraced claims of divine religious power and wealth as our moral foundation. This is the point where modern poverty, war and hunger starts – a point in time where the power of politicians and corporations had its infancy. But the flame of natural justice has never been totally extinguished. Its

Architectural politics in Kindelbrueck.

inalienable power still resides and lives at the heart of our humanity. It is the ember that ignites the fire we feel within our breast when we witness an injustice and it is the root of our just rage. It is as natural and inalienable to us as the air we need to breath. Natural justice is the anger that bursts in our hearts when we feel the jackboot on our necks. Kindelbrueck was also special because it was a distant, hard to defend frontier town. This meant that the normal royal protection was not available. Between 1550 and 1680, Kindelbrueck practiced a kind of early Pendokratie or PSP (people sharing power). They had up to three mayors and a constantly changing set of councilors.

This gave this frontier town stability and it also made the locals very wealthy. They guarded their independence so fiercely that they missed the industrial revolution. The railway tracks bypassed the town. Communism did the rest – it slowly broke down the local's sense of self-reliance and independence. But the communists were not totally to blame for Kindelbrueck's decline. The locals had already begun to forfeit their independence nearly one hundred years earlier before the communists took power, when they gave up their right to run their own council in the 1850's. From then on they were treated by their council as customers, rather than shareholders. This will be further explored in the book PSP.

# *Size matters*

---

The locals love this postcard view of Kindelbrueck because it shows two towers. The church tower and the Council chambers' own tower. This architectural

Big is Boss!

phenomenon occurs in many small formerly independent towns of the region. The church is usually a little taller than the civic towers, symbolising the supremacy of God. Having given God his dues, the locals showed everyone proudly who was really in charge, by building a potent second symbolic civic tower. So it was clear to all that the burgers were in charge under the guidance of God.

For those of us who believe that history does not teach us anything, I have included a picture from another modern small city which lies at the opposite end of the earth – Penrith, Australia.

The tallest building in town is the Tax office. The second tallest building is a huge shopping mall owned by an international commercial property corporation. The local churches have been reduced to restaurants and the ones that still function have very small congregations.

Big is Boss!

Notably, the three estates are no longer Church, King and Worker. Because, now there are only two! National government and international commerce! Where once we had real power, we, the citizens, have today only a democratic illusion of power. Perhaps we can vote out a really bad government – but on a day-to-day basis we are powerless! We have traded the daily sunshine of self-government for the razzmatazz of a once-every-three-year vote.

The symbolism is clear. Whoever collects our taxes and thus extracts the wealth from our communities is in charge!

Today, Kindelbrueck lies impoverished in the heart of

one of the earth's most wealthy nations, Germany. But what is totally incredible about this story is the fact that the same forces which forged Kindelbrueck still exist today.

But the reason why it is no longer a viable town lies with Germany's economic model of exploitation. This model no longer requires a local presence because the wealth of the city can be extracted remotely.

Politically speaking, should the locals desire to close their walls again and ply an inward-looking economic trade, they would again be independent and wealthy. They did it for almost seven hundred years and against much more brutish opponents. They did it in the past and there is nothing that stops them from doing it again today. Having been the inspiration for PSP, they could again raise themselves, with the help of the modern version of PSP, to a higher level of pride and self worth.

The reason why Kindelbrueck or any similar community anywhere else in the world won't stand economically united is the same everywhere. It is in our nature to be a little jealous of our more successful neighbors and friends and we withdraw our support and buy elsewhere where it is anonymous and cheaper. Being a successful local in Kindelbruecks' dialect is called "Ereichern" which means to hoard wealth ill begotten from the exploitation of our neighbors and friends. One of the answers why Kindelbruecks Buergers did stick together for centuries lies in its ancient defense wall. The prospect of buying outside the walls meant certain death and a weakening of the town's defence capabilities.

Today, in the absence of a visible enemy that corrals us behind thick walls, we have lost the communal necessity to unite behind our common good and can instead practice narcissistic ambitions. But we have let the enemy in, and it is eating what little prosperity is left of Kindelbrueck, so small towns fall silently into disrepair and slip into spiritual, communal, real poverty and despair.

As a by-note: one must understand that ancient cities were using restrictive trade, markets and tariffs to destroy fledgling farm-based industries to maintain their monopolies and to keep the costs of raw materials low. But this was only a small part of the whole picture. At a time when dumbing-down was a deliberate policy to keep people servile, the cities were the only place where relative freedom and learning was available.

We still do the same today. We impose restriction on trade to protect us from the competition of poor countries to maintain our unsustainable high standards of living. But we are never confronted with the reality of our actions. We can extract wealth with a remote control and easily deceive ourselves into feeling good about our economic aggressions. We actually manage to kill poor people by the millions every year, which is unpardonable even by the darkest standard of ancient city societies. Cities were also the places where revolutionary ideals could take hold and spread. However, today the destruction of city rights has once again made the *Buerger* subservient and powerless.

The rise and subjugation of free cities is a lesson we

should remember as we go into the future. Today's small cities still have the opportunity to rekindle self-sustainable economic independence that is based on natural justice and can stand on its own feet. But it takes courage and a realisation of how our economic system works and a better system of governance.

Size matters if we want to create a peaceful world. Humanity has only two options to end poverty. We can downsize corporations or cluster together in small city-state-like economically self-serving, self-reliant units that interconnect sensibly with the outside. The process of recognising the size of an economic unit is foreign to our way of life. But size is a vital factor in the creation and distribution of power. If a thing becomes too big, then it strangles competition. Too small and it is unable to provide individuals with enough profits to sustain human life.

If something is dragged over long distances then it become inefficient (Sun Tzu, the art of war. c. 544—496 BC). If something is not distributed widely enough then it becomes dangerously scarce. An easy way to understand this concept is found in determining the right size and location of a hospital. If it is too far away from the majority of the population, then transport costs devour the budget, resulting in poor service to the community. If they are located too close together, then they again devour too many resources due to excess staff and infrastructure costs.

An interesting size-related fraud can also be found in Free Trade where unequal competition squashes local livelihoods in favor of stock market profits. Just because we can deceive emerging, weak and failing states easily through Free Trade and World/Development Bank obligations it does not mean that we have the moral right to cause misery and pain to their populations.

Right sizing is important and an integral part of natural justice. It is central and essential to every political argument and a key element in almost every deception.

The imbalance of power between individual people and the organised power of gigantic, immortal corporation must be seen as a core factor in creating and maintaining a denial of human rights, which is the essence of perpetual poverty. If we can achieve nothing other than the downsizing of corporate power back to a human scale, then we will have begun to end the perpetual cycle of poverty, hunger and war.

# The power-sharing oxymoron

————

Real power is always a congregation of overwhelming ideological and intangible forces. The examples are all around us in nature, politics, business, sports and play.

In political parties, ascending leaders persuade, cajole, blackmail, fight, make deals and go to bed with sub-slime creatures to win power. Elephants use their size and strength to push down trees. Business uses the stock market to build enough financial power to squash their weaker opponents. Even fair-minded athletes fights with all the tools of science at their disposal to win.

But these are vastly different types of power. They divide into natural power and congregated power. Natural power applies to sport, animals and nature's ferocity. Congregated power, on the other hand, is produced when people meet and join in a common cause. These causes can be benevolent or vicious. Benevolently-congregated power might be found in a social or sports club which is built and held together because like-minded people choose to spent time and money in their club. This type of power congregation is benevolent until another factor emerges. Size! A small bowling and social club might turn over a few million per year. Most of its profits are used to supply cheap food and drink to members and guests. Profit also maintains their bowling facilities. But when a club becomes too big, like the fabulous Penrith Leagues Club, then they become predators and begin to take over smaller clubs.

The same size-related pattern emerges in business. Small businesses by themselves are benevolent. They employ people and are beautifully inefficient and wasteful. They have a social conscience and often contribute to building better communities. They also are often more green, because their neighbours enforce a higher level of environmental community standards.

Then along comes a group of power- and money-hungry corporate business people. They build momentum by spinning a yarn of riches, fortunes and fame. They beg, steal and borrow about half a million to list their company on the stock market. Before and during this process, they find financially-strong backers who buy into their spin and become majority shareholders (at a hugely discounted price). After the float, on paper at least, fortunes and profits have already been made. Then, as the business model is rolled out, market share is won as they overpower the smaller local businesses by opening category killer shops and warehouses. They then begin to drown out their smaller competitors' messages by dominating the advertising space in their category. Ridiculously low offers follow and flow until their competitors are starved of sales and forced to fold.

Then prices rise to new heights as the consumers are blackmailed into buying their overpriced goods and services. At the same time, producers and small manufacturers can't sell their products any more because their wholesale customers have shut shop. Cost prices are driven down. Raw material producers are forced to cut wages to below subsistence levels which destroys the integrity of their industry. The timber industry is a case in point!

If we want to live in a harmonious world, then we have to find ways to limit power. We have to build social mechanisms which allow small local businesses to fight the bigger players.

I have tested and adjusted many such mechanisms, and found PSP (people sharing power) to be one of the most robust and universally useful social tools.

Rather than explaining the working of a PSP, which is done in the book *PSP*, let me deal here with power struggle instead.

PSPs help in sharing power between unequal groups of people. They are a mechanism which can allow local rich and poor to live peacefully side by side. Over time, PSPs help to spread opportunities more equally.

Unequal distribution of wealth is a fact we have to live with. We need to find ways to help ordinary people to keep more profit produced by their own labour. As this happens, the opportunities to economically exploit poor people diminish. I postulate that, as the logical extension, excessive wealth will over time become less meaningful, as the world's local incomes become more widely dispersed.

To underline my argument we need to remind ourselves that money is actually stored labour. Someone explained it to me this way: take a hamster which is often seen with its cheeks stretched to bursting point by grain. It hoards the grain knowing that winter is approaching. If it did not hoard grain, it would simply perish in the coming winter. But, come spring time – when seeds are in abundance – any grain left over after winter becomes irrelevant to the hamster. However, our current system takes the leftover grain and turns it into extra money. So it does not get consumed. It actually grows in size and strength.

In our system, stored labour becomes money which is used to build monopolies which, through the exclusion and exploitation of the powerless poor, increases profits. Our monetary system is unnatural and kills between twenty and thirty million people every year.

When we talk about economic growth, and income per capita, India had one of the world's fastest growing economies in 2011. The average per capita income was a few dollars per person per day higher than its neighbor Bangladesh. But averages lie, because the wealthy lifted this figure too high. Proof was that in 2012, 42% (a huge improvement on previous figures) of Indian children were malnourished – a figure worse than in sub-Saharan countries with zero or negative growth.

Economics does not count human values such as the increase or decline in the number of breadwinner able to house, feed and educate their families. Instead, it shows how we have extracted money from the rich as well as from the starving and the poor. Economic growth is a smiling mask that hides the ugly face of starvation and death. The UN's human development index also showed that poverty grew while profits soared in 2011. So rather than the "invisible hand theory" trickling down money, like crumbs falling down from the table of the wealthy, it instead shows how it sucks the food from the begging bowls of the starving.

So, what does that have to do with your personal sense of outrage when an injustice is done? To be blunt, we have forgotten, while following our hedonistic desires, that our forebears did not only wall themselves in behind city walls to keep enemies out, but also to keep prosperity and happiness in!

The next lesson is even more unpalatable because our sense of individualism is contrary to our own well-being. Prestige and social elitism aside, just consider the costs of building a nice communal swimming pool. They are insignificant per person when compared to the costs of building a swimming pool in every backyard. We are also social creatures and love the company and admiration of others. So, next time you contemplate buying a home gym or swimming pool, stop and think what a wonderful gym or pool your local council could provide... if only you had a real say in how your town is run!

It is self-evident that communal property is cheap and even makes a profit that reduces our council's running costs. As a positive side effect, communal property also reduces our reliance on outside finance. Outside finance essentially sucks the profits of our daily labour out of our pocket – out of our towns and into the pockets of a very small, super wealthy minority. Making the wealthy wealthier is no crime. But the re-investing of their profits creates an ever growing, increasingly stronger vacuum suction effect, which ultimately sucks the wealth from the world's most needy and contributes to increased poverty, starvation and death.

But we have alternatives. If we spend and borrow money locally wherever possible, our town's fortunes would quickly improve and, as a byproduct, we would eventually reduce world poverty.

To underpin my argument, I offer the following scenario: it involves two families who have fixed income. Imagine that a child was born into the first family which owns two houses. The second child is also born on the same day to the tenants, who are renting the spare house from the first family. If both children were to die sixty years later, the child who grew up with the proceeds of the collected rent would die richer, whereas the child of the tenants would die poorer. This simplistic view is underpinned by statistics. Most of the rich die rich or richer and most of the poor stay poor.

It is a simple principle that profits flow towards the rich. If the rich happen to be your neighbors, then there is little harm in that. But if these riches are withdrawn from your community and end up in someone else's coffers, somewhere else on this earth, then that clearly is a form of exploitation that will eventually harm you and your neighbors. The very rich can use their power to harm our communities.

This phenomenon finds especially evil outlets in globalisation and free trade. Factually, the only thing that is free about our dishonestly named free trade system is the deaths and misery they cause and I am not being glib with this statement. In the past, we had to wage war to profit from other people's honest toil. We did it through trade, slavery, colonialism and outright war. Today, we starve 11 million people to death annually and we can do it simply and cleanly by playing the stock market. Our weapons of choice are exploitation and economic wars waged by technology and monopolies and under the guise of free trade. Because we do not have to wage a bloody war, these deaths are free! They cost us nothing and seem of no moral or physical consequence to us.

We should rename our large corporations and the stock market to reflect what they actually do. If we kill, we are labeled killers. If we rape, we are rapists. By applying the same logic to shareholders of a monopoly should we not more honestly call them 'raiders' and their activities 'plunder by corporate trade'? Is their behavior not war-like? How do we distinguish between killing in war and killing by denying people the opportunity to sustain themselves?

If someone profits from the stock market does not someone else lose their money, livelihood or both? Is a corporate shareholder not actually an active participant in an economic war? Did Bin Laden perhaps target the World Trade Centre because he saw big business as the enemy of Islam and the creator of intractable poverty, starvation and hunger deaths?

I believe that we need to rethink our relationship with

large, aggressive corporate entities! For example, the stock market system of today has turned into a blatant money laundering machine. It whitewashes more money than casinos! It plays with humanity's fortunes and gives an air of respectability to gambling and militaristic economic aggression.

Shares were invented to reduce investment risk and to reduce hardship when enterprises failed. Initially, shareholders would pool their resources to accomplish large-scale projects or to diffuse risk in overland or sea trade and share risks when growing crops. To have a share in a ship meant that, should the ship sink, the shareholder only lost the value of their share and would not be totally bankrupted. A farmer might have placed his crop on the commodity market to ensure that he can get at least his seed and ploughing costs back, should his crop fail.

Shares were meant to ease hardship. Without wanting to overlook the double standards of the Victorian age it is an interesting by-note to remember that right up to Victorian times, money earned while asleep was considered dirty money by the Vatican. Earlier, however the Medicis found a way to lend money without charging interest, by simply asking a commission for services rendered and thus circumventing the religious objections until they became normal behavior. Usury was frowned upon in christian religious circles to lend money for interest and regarded as a dishonest means of earning a living. Only money earned during your waking hours, by the biblical sweat of your brow, was morally rightfully yours to keep. Ironically Islamic banks too have managed not to charge interest which is forbidden under Sharia law. They avoid the usury by sharing profit and loss, (*Mudharabah*), safekeeping (*Wadiah*), joint-venture (*Musharakah*), cost plus (*Murabahah*), and leasing (*Ijar*).

If we decide to cast a moral doubt on stock markets, should we not rename then? Would a more appropriate name better show their naked aggression? What name would adequately describe their actions?

In 'middle evil' times they would be clearly described as a raiding party on 24-hour lookout for loot! Markets and shareholders alike are no better than pirates or mercenaries of yore – hired guns that aim their inexhaustible financial weapons at the technologically underdeveloped and unaware to extract the highest possible profits. Their boardrooms are nothing more than councils of war; their executives hired killers and the shareholders profiteers.

Call them what you like – if your own actions were to deprive a single person systematically of food, then you would be rightly named a killer and your financiers and backers willing accomplices. Today, as you read this, we have stood by and witnessed the killing of 20,000 people through systematic starvation. And these figures do not include preventable diseases and destabilised countries that wage war, due to our economic actions and interferences.

What really surprises me is that not more acts of terrorism are waged against us as civilians. Are we not the beneficiaries of economic exploitation? Do we not buy stuff at ridiculously low prices? Is this not the point where a great paradox develops? We, the consumer classes, profit from our economic system of plunder by trade. Is it not reasonable to call ourselves accomplices to economically-initiated killings? Can we honestly justly claim to be innocent Mitleufer (blind followers)?

Linking acts of terrorism and unrest in general to poverty or oppression is integral to the human condition. So there can be no question that this link exists. For example, super star terrorists, like Bin Laden in his earlier days, show that their malcontent stems from social injustice. In his case, the Saudis were alleged to have mistreated poor Muslims and Bin Laden took up their case and sullied his family's good business name and measures were allegedly taken to have him relinquish his passport and Saudi nationality. Having hit a brick wall to assist poor Muslims when he was in his thirties, he turned to radical Islamic teachings that promised the restoration of Islamic glory days and a restoration of former Islamic Ottoman caliph territories. Restoring the seven Islamic pillars:

- Walayah - Guarding the faith to which a believer lovingly submits

- Tawhid -Believing in just One God

- Salah -Regular Prayer

- Paying -12.5% of income to welfare and Charity

- Sawm -Obtaining divine truth through Fasting-

- Hajj -Pilgrimage – Literally fleeing from devils and oppressors

- Jihad -Struggle to preserve the inner peace of the faith avoiding provocation whilst preferring to be a pacifist.

So Bin Laden has two faces. One devout and the other the strategic terror war lord. The devout face was used to find willing fighters longing to cleanse the Islamic world of infidel business exploitation and to restore peace, prosperity and harmony to Muslims, whilst the war lord face was used coldly to stategise war and murder using religious fever as a weapon of terror.

Bin Laden the son of a wealthy business man was brought up living a priviliged life but turned to radical Islam, finding justification for his reign of terror in the teachings of the radical Islamic Brotherhood, which turned the Islamic piller of Zakah "Charity" and interdependence into a Jihad or "Struggle" which would normally be an an inner struggle. But in Bin Ladin's case it, was turned into an external struggle and terrorism to defend the pillars of islam by confronting the enemies of the faith. Namly western infidels who's busines practices encurraged exploitation instaed of Islamic interdependence and charity. This potent mix of religious righteousness and blood-lust was and still is a fearsome weapon of mass destruction and one that cannot simply be defeated by a show of military force. In 2012, ten years after 9/11, the fighting spirit of the terrorists has not diminished. At times they are down, but so far they have never been taken totally out of the war game.

At the beginning of the *War Against Terrorism,* war correspondents prophesied that we will have to sit down and talk to al-Qaeda after a long and bloody war. In January 2012, this is exactly what happened when al-Qaeda opened a negotiating office in Kabul whist the US lead forces withdrew defeated from Afghanistan.

Had they gone in, checkbooks blazing, winning hearts and minds, the war would have been won for a fraction of the cost, a fraction of the misery, deaths and destabilization that it caused. You can convert someone at point blank whilst the gun is pointed and loaded, growing ever more resentful and bitter as you get war-weary, but you can only turn your back on a hostile people when you win hearts and minds through selfless generosity.

When I say that we are complicit in the maintenance of poverty and imply that we have to restore simple human dignities to the world's poor I also have to set things straight. An hour before I wrote these lines, I was driven through Chennai by a taxi for the equivalent of $7 – including waiting time of a few hours and a trip of about ten kilometers. I purchased two travel bags and a wallet from a two by two meter shop that sells leather goods seconds and factory overruns. I asked the kind driver to wait for me. I made my way over the rough shoulder of Chennai's Grand Trunk Road which is falling into disrepair before it is even fully commissioned due to dodgy bribery-riddled building practices. The leading political party in the days when the road and some flyovers were built took so many bribes that there was little money left to complete the entire project. After they lost office, you could not get a lawyer for weeks, because the new ruling party had made good on a promise to investigate all lab-grab cases where poor locals were forced to sell their land for peanuts or no money at all to party cronies and their families.

When the cronies foolishly held a rally, the newly elected party sent in the police and arrested them by the dozen and put them on remand row like chooks on a charcoal grill. The ones that escaped the net fought hard to find  lawyers who could track down the victims of their land-grabs and offer them compensation in the hope of avoiding jail time. Then there is the issue of the missing pavement stones which were delivered, stacked by the roadside for months, if not years, but were never installed because there was no money left for wages after bribes had been paid The beautiful hand cut granite pavement stones naturally vanished into private yards during the balmy Chennai nights.

Leading into the leather shop was a sewerage line which was only partially covered with thin concrete slabs, which emitted a hefty stench and attracted mosquito which carry all types of diseases which run rampant in Chennai. On the way to the dimly lit leather goods store, climbing up a few steps, built to elevate the shops above the floods during the monsoon season, I noticed a beggar settling in for the night on a small landing above the steps. He settled down, his back turned towards the road as he pulled a thin brine-stained cloth to cover himself as he curled into a fetal position. I quietly passed the skeletal fetus-shaped man, who was hoping to get a good and safe night's sleep, rising again with the sun, hoping to get some day-labour work tomorrow and a small amount of food money for pay.

I slipped into the shop and eyed a shopkeeper astonished to see a customer. I bought two excellent travel bags and some purses as presents for long-neglected relatives. It came to five thousand two hundred rupees, about $125. When I asked the shopkeeper for the price, I asked what he could accept and did not push hard for a discount, which is the local custom. His entire shop inventory was worth about five hundred dollars. From this, after paying for goods, rent and electricity he fed and clothed his family. Five hundred was about the price I paid for the camera, a tool of my trade in optics, which I always carried in my pocket.

One of the travel bags was made from buffalo hide and was what we call in the retail trade a shop-minder – an item which stays on the shelf until it is nearly an antique, stubbornly defying all efforts to offload it to a hapless customer. I recognized the bag's style from airport shops where something similar was sold for over one thousand dollars.

So what is the point of this tale? Simply this. Gandhi said that there is no enjoyment in buying something that the ordinary man cannot afford. True to form, I felt that this purchase, which cost more than my drivers was paid in a month, gave me no joy. I had bought some luxury items at a fair price (in his worldview), which comparably were super bargains in the western world, but still unattainable for the locals. I felt like the proverbial golden goose ready to be plucked, as bystanders appeared and crowded around me out of thin air and watched where I kept my wallet and gasped when I handed over a month's wages for a few leather items. Throats have been cut for less and I felt dumb in the pincer movement between the elated shopkeeper who just sold his store-minder at a good price and the glum faces of the bystanders who saw wads of money change hands. As I left the shop, my driver gave me a friendly nod, waved and gladly took my bags to lighten my load. Then the shopkeeper tapped me on the shoulder and handed me a very nice leather key holder and said "Happy New Year". Smiles all around!

Happiness and contentment are a state of mind and anyone who expects hoards of poor people to invade rich countries is missing the point. Poor people in this case love being Indian. They are warm, graceful and have a ready open smile. They could think of no better and happier place on earth than India, but are quick to admit that it would be nice if life would be a little less tough and even nicer if there was a bit more food to go around and perhaps a safe shelter to call home. Not much to ask for, really! As to the traveling bags: one of them I'll use proudly, like most things I own, for decades to remind me of this simple truth. The other travel bag was intended to serve in a micro-business experiment aimed at delivering specs to poor villagers. So, my conscience was almost clear, but I still wish I had bought items that the local could afford and probably will next time. Gandhi's private secretary, V. Kalyanam (now in his mid-nineties and still a workaholic and sharp as a tack), who was with Gandhi until his death, said of him in a flier that summarises Gandhi's achievements: "His greatness lay in doing what everybody could do but did not care to do. He traveled III (Third) class because there was no IV(Fourth) Class." He then quoted as Gandhi's highest principal: "I hate privilege and monopoly. Whatever cannot be shared with the masses is taboo to me." Gandhi pleaded with his followers: "I do not want you to live like saints in diapers. I only ask you to be less selfish, less greedy, less money-mad and less self-centered. Be more kind, more honest, more friendly, more brotherly and more public spirited."

It is also worth noting that begging is not as widespread in India as one might think. Sure, you get the odd cute smiling four year old grabbing your hand and not letting go until you part with some loose change, or the odd young single mum shunned by her family begging at the car window. But mostly it a process of negotiation. An employee might say that life is tough because three have to live on one dollar a day. No doubt it's tough, but even more so, if the business pays too much, sinks into the red and fails – with everyone losing their jobs. It is tough all around and when running an enterprise in developing countries it's equally tough and spiritually exhausting on the first world managers and owners. But make no mistake. Wage and bargaining is the preferred process to exchange values, not begging! I do this, if you can do or give me that; if it's fair we both wiggle our heads in the typical Chennai way that only Chennaits understand to mean the same as a loud OK and the deal is done. You give what you can and I'll only ask for what I really need. Poor people are not ignorant, heartless or stupid. Many are even quite well educated and I have hired some that have a seriously higher IQ than I fancy for myself. It's just that many have never had a break that got them off the poverty treadmill.

The poor don't want charity. The want opportunity and a fair go at living life free of hunger and deprivation. We should keep our missionary zest firmly locked in history books, because the poor already have tons of spirituality and enjoy more laughs on a day than I get in a year. It just would be nice to think that the poor no longer have to feed the girls of the family last, so that the boys grow strong and able to work hard to support their extended family. Again, the poor know how to live and fend for themselves, but they do need opportunities to help themselves. It's very bit like Martin Luther King's saying: "It's cruel to tell a poor man to pull himself up by his boot straps, when he has no boots."

Terrorists have figured this out a long time ago. Not always are they just motivated by misplaced religious zeal, many also do not view our economic actions as innocent, but point to our guilt by association, as the ultimate beneficiaries of economic plunder by trade which is the key tool in creating and maintaining intractable poverty.

US president Bush quite rightly called his actions against terrorists a *"War on terrorism"*, because ironically we are the instigators of the economic war and plunder by trade.

Iran demonstrates why we are heading into a very dangerous future. Dangerous technology can today be transferred via an e-mail in seconds and developing nations are every bit as smart as the rest of the world. Being at the bum-end of our economic actions, they also instinctively understand what is being done to them. Iran, being a religious dictatorship, is dangerous because they seek the protection of nuclear weapons as a force against our economic hegemony and against plunder by trade which violates at least one of the Islamic pillars.

Again the same fundamentalist Islamic extremist tactics used by Bin Laden are being practiced by Iran. What makes us nervous is that the shoe that fitted Bin Laden also fits Iran, although on a much larger scale and with the added gravitas of a state war machine and an emerging nuclear menace which ironically funded by our consumption of petroleum products, behind them. Once the USA funded Bin Laden's fledgling Taliban to fight the Russians, now we do it again at a huge scale, funding Iran. Again one wonders if a cheque book-led diplomatically-built relationship with troubled countries might not be a more potent initiative than military threats and interventions. But impoverished, impotent folk crushed under Western economic might are also crushed by the wealthy and powerful within each desolate country that is controlled by an elite that is quite happy to be filthy rich and watch their own multitudes starve and perhaps find it easy to blame an external enemy to give the poor someone outside their country to hate. In the end the Taliban provided schools and aid, that won them the admiration of a multitude of followers. If it works for the Taliban why would peace initiatives ties to aid not work for the west?

It was incomprehensible that during the NY trade centre bombing, Palestinians, celebrated and danced in the street. Shaking our heads (even though our media is politically tainted) in total disbelief, we saw people on TV, dancing as the twin towers smouldered and collapsed. It is perhaps this image that led to a blinded hatred of all things Muslim that followed.

I believe they danced because they saw a heavy blow being dealt to their opponents' economic war machinery. To them, the world trade centre was the nerve hub of an economical weapon used against Islamic principles. Our business institution, which we created to bring freedom and free trade, instead is seen as the harbinger of death, destruction, poverty and Un-Islamic values.

It is too easy to liken terrorism simply to religious hate crimes. Terrorism that declares war on billions of people has to have a more grave reason, be it a religious belief that aspires to rule over a territory or economic reasons. Or be it a kind of envy that detests the opulent lifestyle of the developed world and detests the low prices achieved for the produce of developing nations, which keeps them running hard on the hamster-wheel of poverty.

Economic, political and cultural disenfranchisement all play a powerful part in kindling terrorism. Because two thirds of all terrorist are young middle class educated people one can not totally blame poverty as the sole cause of terrorism. But it is definably one of the main ingredients which fuels discontent. It is appropriate to also introduce a denial of Natural Justice into this potent mix. The simple believe that an existence free of oppression is an undeniable birthright is surly another powerful trigger to turn to terrorism when this just primal urge is oppressed.

This is what Ken McDonald—Britain's most senior criminal prosecutor thinks about this issue:

*"London is not a battlefield. Those innocents who were murdered...were not victims of war. And the men who killed them were not, as in their vanity they claimed on their ludicrous videos, 'soldiers'. They were deluded, narcissistic inadequates. They were criminals. They were fantasists. We need to be very clear about this. On the streets of London there is no such thing as a war on terror. The fight against terrorism on the streets of Britain is not a war. It is the prevention of crime, the enforcement of our laws, and the winning of justice for those damaged by their infringement."* Wikipedia 2009

I let you decide if either side can claim the unassailable moral high ground in this conflict. But any way I look at it, the victims of terrorism are not faceless. They are someone's fathers, mothers, sisters and brothers and their pain is real and their complicity in economic or religious wrongdoings tenuous. In other words they are victims of crime that is wearing the false mask of religion or that of the freedom fighter. Simple criminals by another name.

You can not win a just conflict or undo an injustice by inflicting violence and pain on others. This cause of action puts you right into the corner of criminality.

The danger we face is namely this: as we become technologically more advanced, our destructive technologies, such as bio-weapons are cheaper to manufacture and easy to deploy. It is not inconceivable that some day soon large-scale acts of terrorism are likely to succeed because we have lost, for a brief moment, a vital technology to our opponents.

If we see our economic actions clearly for what they are, we have a chance to call an economic cease-fire. We should make an honest attempt to clearly name our corporations *Economic-raiders* and honestly try to repair the collateral damage we have inflicted. We must begin to view our economic actions as tactics of war and consider if the profits we, as the consumer-class, derive from it are worth the terror, instability and fears we suffer as a consequence. The best policy to avoid strife with your neighbors is to ensure that their bellies are full and that the profit of their labour stays with them!

I hark back to the Kindelbrueck example, where power is mostly local and diffused rather than in the hands of an elite few. Simple city planning and diffusion of power derived from taxes would go a long way to defuse national aggressions.

The worst thing we can do is to accelerate our profit growth, to reinvest profit and to notch-up our economic war machinery to the point where it will bring us all to total destruction. All it takes is a rogue state, organisation or technologically-savvy individual to deploy nuclear weapons and the still active arsenals in both the old soviet and the western blocs will blow us all to kingdom come.

We all forget that, after the end of the cold war, neither the Soviets nor the Americans disarmed. We still have massive nuclear and biological fire-power, which can destroy us all several times over.

We are living in a world of make-believe, when in reality we are dancing on the edge of an abyss. Now, more than ever, we need to find the resolve to act and bring our system of economic terror and war to an end.

The current trend of terrorism has a strong element of deranged fanaticism about it, which is a prelude to common war. Terrorists dream of rectifying an injustice by infliction another injustice which is why Gandhi said that *"an eye for an eye will only reap blind hate"*.

So is there any point of living in fear of terrorists? No, because they will strike at random, at any time and at any place. The point of terrorism is to terrorise! So, when we buy into the fear generated by terrorism, the terrorists have already won.

To truly fight a just war against an oppressor, one must respect the rights of every individual first, and then proceed to seek restorative justice. This is the only path to peace.

Just consider what would have happened in South Africa had Tutu not defused the racial revenge powder keg by creating a Truth and Justice Commission where grievances could be heard and perpetrators pardoned. A descent into dark days of butchery was only narrowly avoided. ⚙

# *Symbolism*

---

**PSP** people sharing power is a mechanism which reduces corruption and produces economically sound and fair power-sharing decisions. Far from being an oxymoron or delusional it is a practical method to govern without inequality.

The PSP logo symbolises that cooperation and power

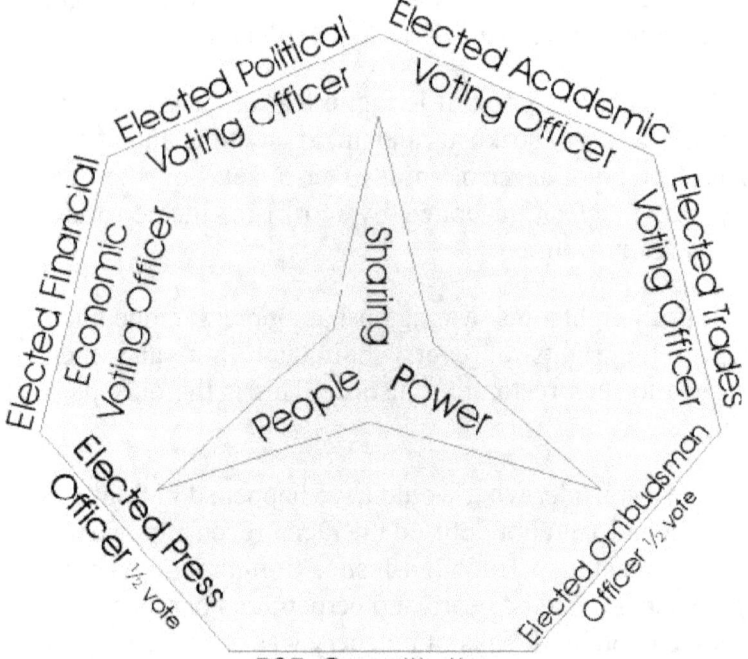

sharing are the foundation of a peaceful and just society.

The three-legged cross can also symbolise the three forms of human power or three modern day estates of man – the power of natural justice, the power of government and the power of the people, their economic output and their combined consumption.

Flag during India's epic independence struggle

Indians used the spinning wheel to symbolise that individual economic actions can topple empires.

The spinning wheel was adopted by Gandhi after he used locally made cloth to break the English dominated textile trade.

Gandhi in his trade-mark self-made dhoti cloth.

Gandhi began to wear his simple self-made, locally spun cloth-wrap to make a political point; namely, to show the British that simple economic actions can break even the strongest empire. It was also intended to show India's poor that they have a voice – when they act collectively.

The cloth also symbolised his sympathy with the desperately poor.

Like many ascetic leaders before him in eastern and western religions, he believed that public leaders should have no personal possessions and he firmly believed that leaders should sustain themselves from the good their leadership creates.

Gandhi said that a few determined people can change the course of history and modern day Satyagraha followers in India still wrestle with gigantic forces using little else than truth, determination and non-violence.

Just a few hours before I wrote this closing paragraph in 2012, a prominent Gandhian on an anti corruption Satyagraha campaign was attacked with black ink. The victim's only good eye copped the full force of the ink. His followers wrestled with the attacker, tempers flared and he got a beating before being handed over to police. The first words the Gandhian said were: "I am sorry that my attacker was beaten up. It should not have happened. Let the law deal with my assailant. But I will continue to fight corruption to the death ...even if the next attack is with a bullet! " What a powerful Satyagraha action!

Non-violence has turned an attack into a media frenzy that shone the light into the black heart of India's greed and corruption.

Imaging what you could achieve if you had the Satyagraha's truth strength in your arsenal. But first you must go through the rigours of finding your foundation in non-violence and an unassailable truth. Otherwise you are just clowning around, making even like-minded people cringe with embarrassment. The one thing that Gandhi tough above all was that you as an individual are a single but powerful force when you act morally against injustice. Be it a simple ethical purchase or an organised resistance against an injustice. All peace loving religions and just ideologies share the golden rule of Ethical of Reciprocity: Do unto others as you want them do unto you.

We should cerebrate the fact that so many religions, politics and ideologies nurture the good within us and rejoice that all are enlightened derivatives of the same powerful but peaceful uniquely human genetic imprint; Natural Justice.

www.ingramcontent.com/pod-product-compliance
Lightning Source LLC
Chambersburg PA
CBHW070119010626
45794CB00012B/343